D1071004

12/15

Aaron,

This is one of our favorite Psalms 91 because God insures us of His Care and Protection. We really have nothing to fear because God Is with Me. Emmanuel!

We Love You So Much
Pop and Nan
La Place

GOD'S SHIELD OF PROTECTION FOR YOUR FUTURE

PSALM 91

FOR

TEENS

PEGGY JOYCE RUTH
ANGELIA RUTH SCHUM

CHARISMA
HOUSE

Most CHARISMA HOUSE BOOK GROUP products are available at special quantity discounts for bulk purchase for sales promotions, premiums, fund-raising, and educational needs. For details, write Charisma House Book Group, 600 Rinehart Road, Lake Mary, Florida 32746, or telephone (407) 333-0600.

PSALM 91 FOR TEENS by Peggy Joyce Ruth and
    Angelia Ruth Schum
Published by Charisma House
Charisma Media/Charisma House Book Group
600 Rinehart Road
Lake Mary, Florida 32746
www.charismahouse.com

This book or parts thereof may not be reproduced in any form, stored in a retrieval system, or transmitted in any form by any means—electronic, mechanical, photocopy, recording, or otherwise—without prior written permission of the publisher, except as provided by United States of America copyright law.

Unless otherwise noted, all Scripture quotations are from the New American Standard Bible, copyright © 1960, 1962, 1963, 1968, 1971, 1972, 1973, 1975, 1977, 1995 by The Lockman Foundation. Used by permission. (www.Lockman.org)

Scripture quotations marked MEV are from the Modern English Version. Copyright © 2014 by Military Bible Association. Used by permission. All rights reserved.

Scripture quotations marked NIV are from the Holy Bible, New International Version®, NIV®. Copyright © 1973, 1978, 1984, 2011 by Biblica, Inc.™ Used by permission of Zondervan. All rights reserved worldwide.

Scripture quotations marked NLT are taken from the Holy Bible, New Living Translation. Copyright © 1996, 2004, 2007, 2013 by Tyndale House Foundation. Used by permission of Tyndale House Publishers, Inc. Carol Stream, Illinois 60188. All rights reserved.

Scripture quotations marked KJV are from the King James Version of the Bible.

Copyright © 2015 by Peggy Joyce Ruth and Angelia Ruth Schum
All rights reserved

Special thanks to editors: John Williams, Stephanie Lykins, Roberta Wescott, Barbara Dycus, Brandi Bunch, Ann Johnson, Donna Johnson, and Margie Ayala.

Cover design by: Justin Evans

Visit the author's website at www.peggyjoyceruth.org.

Library of Congress Cataloging-in-Publication Data:
Ruth, Peggy Joyce.
  Psalm 91 for teens / by Peggy Joyce Ruth and Angelia Ruth Schum. -- 1 [edition].
      pages cm
  Includes bibliographical references and index.
  ISBN 978-1-62998-227-4 (trade paper : alk. paper) -- ISBN

978-1-62998-228-1 (e-book)
  1. Bible. Psalms, XCI--Meditations. 2. Bible. Psalms, XCI--
Meditations. 3. Christian teenagers--Religious life. I. Title.
  BS145091st .R89 2015
  223'.206--dc23
                                        2015020174

While the author has made every effort to provide accurate
Internet addresses at the time of publication, neither the
publisher nor the author assumes any responsibility for
errors or for changes that occur after publication.

Some names and identifying details have been changed to
protect the privacy of individuals

This publication is translated in Spanish under the title
Salmo 91 para jóvenes, copyright © 2015 by Peggy Joyce
Ruth and Angelia Ruth Schum, published by Casa Creación,
a Charisma Media company. All rights reserved.

First edition

15 16 17 18 19 — 987654321
Printed in the United States of America

CONTENTS

PSALM
91

He who dwells in the shelter of the Most High
shall abide under the shadow of the Almighty.
I will say of the LORD, "He is my refuge and my fortress,
my God in whom I trust."

Surely He shall deliver you from the snare of the hunter
and from the deadly pestilence.
He shall cover you with His feathers,
and under His wings you shall find protection;
His faithfulness shall be your shield and wall.
You shall not be afraid of the terror by night,
nor of the arrow that flies by day;
nor of the pestilence that pursues in darkness,
nor of the destruction that strikes at noonday.
A thousand may fall at your side
and ten thousand at your right hand,
but it shall not come near you.
Only with your eyes shall you behold
and see the reward of the wicked.

Because you have made the LORD, who is my refuge,
even the Most High, your dwelling,
there shall be no evil befall you,
neither shall any plague come near your tent;
for He shall give His angels charge over you
to guard you in all your ways.
They shall bear you up in their hands,
lest you strike your foot against a stone.
You shall tread upon the lion and adder;
the young lion and the serpent you shall trample underfoot.

Because he has set his love upon Me,
therefore I will deliver him;
I will set him on high, because he has known My name.
He shall call upon Me, and I will answer him;
I will be with him in trouble,
and I will deliver him and honor him.

With long life I will satisfy him
and show him My salvation.

—MEV

SWITCH PLAY

THE BOOK *PSALM 91: Military Edition* includes a famous story about a soldier who had Psalm 91 come into his life unexpectedly.[1] It is one of my favorite stories. This lieutenant was literally saved from being shot in the heart because of a Bible in his front shirt pocket. He was flabbergasted when he opened the little Bible and found that the bullet had stopped at Psalm 91.

The story below is another one of my favorites. It's from a teen about someone receiving the book *Psalm 91* unexpectedly.

We were in Baton Rouge, Louisiana. This place has some of the longest-lasting red lights I have ever seen. People would turn their cars off while sitting there. This left us (two vanloads of students on spring break) with plenty of spare time to do … nothing. So as I was looking out the window at one of the many never-ending stoplights, I saw this woman in her car reading a book. And as I took a closer look at the book, I realized it was a New Age type of self-help book. I often have ideas that can get me in trouble if anything goes wrong, and this time did not fail to produce such an idea as this.

I rolled down my window and looked at this woman reading this book that I deemed unworthy of having her eyes laid upon it, and I took aim. With what? A *Psalm 91* book. Praise God, the window was down just far enough for me to get this book in. As it went sailing into her car, it smacked the self-help book straight out of her hands and then disappeared to the floorboard of her car. And from the looks of her floorboard, she would never find the book ever again. As the New Age book went flying, the *Psalm 91* book landed square in her lap. It had literally replaced what she was reading!

A look of rage and anger took over the woman's face as she dropped her head to see what had hit her. And I went, "Aw, snap." Thankfully her anger didn't last long. The look on her face quickly turned into excitement and joy as she started screaming, "I have been looking for this book! I can't believe it! I wanted this book!" Her response was loud enough that people in several other cars turned and looked at her. Just then the light turned green and we were off.

I vaguely remember seeing tears coming to her eyes as she opened that book and started to read it as the cars were passing her by. Everyone in our van was turned around in their seats to see this scene unfold. They witnessed with their own eyes how this woman had a God encounter right in the middle of the highway, and no one could quit talking about it. The driver following us saw the incident as well and passed the woman by as she just sat in her car unable to take her eyes off the book that had miraculously flown into her hands.

—KYLE OXFORD

God has unique ways of getting the message of Psalm 91 to people. What a simple but comical way God had of honoring this woman who desired this very book. I'm not sure how you came across this teen edition, but the Psalm 91 message came to me in a unique way as well. Here is my story.

HOW I CAME TO DISCOVER PSALM 91

In my early twenties I started praying and asking God if there was some way for a Christian to be protected from all the evil things that were happening in the world. I feared everything from heart attacks and cancer to car wrecks and terrorism. When I thought of all those things, I would begin to feel more and more anxious. I asked, "Lord, is there any way we can be protected? Can our family be protected?" I was not expecting an answer.

Just minutes after asking that question, I fell asleep, and I had a very vivid dream that I will never forget. In the dream I was in an open field, asking the same question I had prayed earlier: "Is there any way to be protected from all the bad things that are coming on the earth?" In the dream I heard the words: "In your day of trouble call upon Me, and I will answer you..." The words were from Psalm 91, which I had never heard before.

The next day I heard the words "Psalm 91," and I suddenly knew in my heart that whatever was in that psalm was my answer from God. I began turning the pages of my Bible so quickly that I nearly tore them in my haste to find the psalm. It was the answer I had been praying for. I had found the exact words I had dreamed. I was so happy that I cried.

Do you remember the last time you got something you wanted so desperately you couldn't stop thinking about it? Do you remember feeling happy all over—so much so you couldn't quit smiling? That was how I felt when I first turned to Psalm 91 and read it out loud. I was so elated that God had answered my prayer and had shown me a way to conquer my fears. So I started studying Psalm 91 every day.

Then God told me it was not just a promise for me but for all of His people. He urged me to write a book to tell everyone of His promises of protection and to help them get free from fear.

God's promise of protection is for all ages. Of all the lessons we have taught in our years of youth ministry, the Psalm 91 message has been a favorite! It is one of the most important things you will ever learn, so take time now to find Psalm 91 in your Bible. Let's go through it together, uncovering valuable insights as we study this psalm about God's protection.

At the beginning of each chapter we've included a testimony illustrating a verse from Psalm 91. Each of these stories will challenge you to apply the verse right in your own walk with the Lord.

Someone has quipped, "Put the word in you when you don't need it, so when you do need it, it will be there." As you will see in Avery's story in the next chapter, now is the time to get Psalm 91 deep inside you for those times in your life when you will most need these promises.

Think of how absurd it would be for a man to run to his weight set and begin to work out after a thief has broken into his home. It doesn't make sense, and it's no laughing matter when we realize we've waited too late to protect ourselves.

Now is the time to start applying the promises of Psalm 91. Start early in life to equip yourself with a *preventative* approach to the power of God's promises in your life.

—Peggy Joyce Ruth

Chapter 1

WHERE IS YOUR SECRET HIDING PLACE?

*He who dwells in the shelter of the Most High shall
abide under the shadow of the Almighty.*

—Psalm 91:1, MEV

AIRBORNE

It was July Fourth weekend a few years back in Montana. Everything was normal that night…well, normal for the Fourth anyway. My whole family was sitting on a blanket in a park watching the fireworks show— my mom, my dad, my sister and brother, our two dogs, and me. As the fireworks ended, my dad had all of our stuff packed in a little red wagon we brought while simultaneously holding the dogs on a leash, and we began walking back to our car. We had come to the road and were getting ready to cross…but I was a little too impatient to get home. So when my dad signaled us to cross, I took off like an Olympian, except not as fast…or graceful.

Seemingly out of nowhere, I was struck by a red car, which was later reported to be going forty-five miles per hour. Onlookers said I went flying straight up into the air, but I never knew it—it felt like I was on the hood the whole time. The reason I don't know is my eyes were closed, and I couldn't have opened them even if I'd tried. The next thing I knew, I was on the ground! At that time all I could think was, "My family is going to be shocked and scared that I was just hit by a car. I need to calm them down." So I stood up in the blink of an eye and said, "I'm OK! I'm OK!" with a smile on my face.

What wasn't such a big crowd initially seemed to have tripled in size. However, my efforts to keep everyone calm seemed to be in vain, as I could hear murmurs all around me. My mom was rushing to me panicking, and I could hear my dad arguing with the driver of the car that just hit me. When I looked toward the car, I saw that the window was cracked severely and the front was very badly dented. "It felt so smooth just a second ago," I thought to myself.

At this point, my mom was very upset and praying Psalm 91 very loudly. She had the whole family praying, and my sister blurted out, "If God is so powerful, why did this happen?" It really upset me. I scolded her and said, "God is so powerful that when things like this happen, He protects us supernaturally!"

Immediately, to my surprise, the ambulance arrived and I couldn't help but feel it wasn't needed because I felt just fine. All I still wanted to do was go home, but they kept asking me questions to see if I was injured. I answered every question correctly so they said I was fine. But my mom took me to the ER anyway, and I sat there for hours! When I was finally examined, all they could find wrong with me was a scratch on my middle finger and a small head-ache, which barely lasted an hour. My mom insisted on X-rays and tests, and it wasn't until after the doctor came in and told us that nothing was broken that we *finally* went home. I remember telling my mom, "I always knew God had a plan for my life, but He really must have something big planned for me, huh?" And she definitely agreed. I'm thankful every day that God protected me.

—AVERY, AGE 15

This family actively claims the promises of Psalm 91 on a daily basis. This passage is a place they dwell as a family. You can see it in Avery's story. Avery had Psalm 91 deep inside him because he had started memorizing the whole chapter at age four and had it completely memorized by the age of seven. It had become such a part of him that when the accident happened, he said he never felt fear and knew that he was protected even as the car hit him. Avery's mom was shouting, "We have Psalm 91 protection!" as she watched her son go flying through the air like a rag doll and land on his head on the windshield. She prayed this psalm daily over her family, and even in the face of danger, she chose to find that secret place of the Most High.

The front bumper where Avery hit was dented, the windshield had a spiderweb crack all the way across from where Avery's head landed, and the hood had a caved-in dent where he landed before he rolled off the car—and yet God had Avery in the shadow of His protection. It was nothing short of a miracle when you think of the damage Avery did to the car, yet the car didn't do damage to the ninety-pound boy!

HIDING IN GOD

The King James Version of Psalm 91:1 gives us a unique understanding of the *shelter* of the Most High by letting us know it is a *secret* hiding place. It gives us a cozy feeling of having a special place between God and us. God is calling us to a secret place with Him. Think about where you want to be when you need security. I remember when I was a little girl and would wake up in the middle of the night, feeling afraid; I would tiptoe down to my mother and dad's room and very quietly slip into their bed. I would lie there silently, listening to them breathe, feeling cozy and protected. Before I knew it, the fear was gone, and I would be sound asleep.

My parents would often take me and my brother and sister to a lake. There was a wonderful place to fish for perch that very few people knew about, and we loved to fish.

One of those outings proved to be more exciting than most, turning out to be an experience I will never forget. It had been a beautiful day when we started out, but by the time we'd finished fishing and were headed toward the cove with the trotline, the sky had begun to darken. A storm came up on the lake so fast there was no time to get back to the dock. The clouds were black and rolling, lightning was flashing, and drops of rain were falling so hard they stung our skin. Moments later, the rain was joined by marble-sized hail, falling thick and fast.

When I saw the fear in my mother's eyes, I knew we were in danger. But before I had time to wonder what we were going to do, Dad had driven the boat to the rugged shoreline of the only island on the lake. It looked like an abandoned island with absolutely no place to hide from the storm.

In just minutes, Dad had us all on shore and out of the boat. Quickly pulling a canvas tarp out of the bottom of the boat, he knelt down on the ground beside us and pulled that tarp up and over the five of us. The storm raged outside the homemade tent he put over us—the rain beat down, the lightning cracked, the thunder rolled, and the waves crashed on the shore—but all I could think about was how it felt to have my dad's arms around me. As the storm raged on all around us, I experienced a special peace that is hard to explain. In fact, I had never felt so safe and secure in my entire life. I remember thinking I wished the storm would never end! I didn't want anything to spoil the wonderful security I felt there *in our secret hiding place.* I felt so safe in the midst of the storm, I could have stayed there forever.

—PEGGY JOYCE RUTH

GOD IS A *SAFE* PLACE

Looking toward the future and thinking about heading out into the world can be frightening. Now is the best time to find your own personal safe place with God. Maybe you already have a secret place where you feel safe and secure and can talk to Him about what's on your heart. It could be a park or a drive you take in your car or even just your room, but that place always pulls you back in with familiarity and the quiet reassurance that everything will somehow turn out OK.

Physical places can only be what they are—natural protection; they can't keep you safe from everything. Sometimes relationships go bad. Sometimes relationships leave you feeling empty and disappointed. Spending time with the Lord every day before you attempt to develop any other new relationships will save you a lot of pain and heartache. God alone is the only One with whom our hearts are truly safe. Entrust your heart to His gentle hands. Our hearts are never at home until we put them in His care.

RUN TO GOD WITH YOUR HEART

God is a *place* of shelter that will keep you protected. God says that He is the place of real safety from every bad thing you can think of in the whole earth—if you will run to Him. Just as a shepherd fights to protect his sheep, He will fight to protect you. God says He will lift you up and joyfully carry you on His shoulders (Luke 15:5).

Run to God, not with your feet, but with your heart. You are running to God every time you think about Him, every time you tell Him you love Him, every time you work out your problems with His help, every time you make the time to talk to Him. If you believe God is telling you the truth when He says He is a place of safety where you can be protected, then you are ready to start this journey.

Before you step through the gateway into the world around you, be sure you have found your secret hiding place with Him.

CHAPTER 1—JOURNAL

This chapter emphasizes the importance of finding your hiding place with God. Do you have a special place with God where you have experienced His presence and protection?

On the floor of my
room and in the shower
I feel safe to talk to
God aloud.

I MUST LEARN TO TRUST AND TO SAY

I will say of the LORD, "He is my refuge and my fortress, my God in whom I trust."
—**PSALM 91:2**, MEV

OVERPOWERED AND EMPOWERED

One Sunday morning I had gotten out of bed early to get ready for church when I heard a knock. My apartment complex was a peaceful, friendly place, and most unsolicited callers were Girl Scouts selling cookies or people searching for lost cats. I didn't even consider something terrible happening at seven in the morning, so I opened the door. It had only moved a few inches when a large man shoved his way into my apartment and pushed me back through my bedroom door, making it clear that his intention was to harm me. I remember thinking, "Things like this don't happen to me. I must be dreaming."

The man was so much larger and stronger than I was that I knew I couldn't fight him. He pushed me toward my room and pinned me down. We wrestled for about ten minutes. I struggled, but I couldn't break free.

At that point, I didn't know *how* God would deliver me, but I began saying out loud, "Jesus, help me. Jesus, help me." The attacker told me to shut up. I answered back, "I don't know who you are or what you have done, or even if the police are after you, but you need

Jesus. I am going to church today, and you can come." My emotions were hysterical but my spirit was strong.

For a moment, he snapped out of it and looked around, but then his eyes glazed over and his face took on a demonic look, and he tried to pin me down again. I kept calling on Jesus, and the man told me to shut up if I wanted to live. Panicking, I managed to break away and get into the living room, but he caught me again. I told him that there were angels in the room. He looked me in the eye and snapped, "There are demons in this room too." Calling on God, I replied, "Well, my angels are stronger than your demons."

And then, in a moment, he was at a standstill.

I seized that moment of spiritual victory and managed to get out of the apartment to call the police. It had taken forty-five minutes of spiritual battle as he came at me time after time, but I never quit calling out to Jesus and quoting His promises. And each time it would bring confusion and immobility upon him, blocking every attempted attack. The police were able to track him by an earring he lost in the carpet.

Later, after he was apprehended and held in custody, I found out that he had assaulted numerous young women, and I was the only one who had been able to escape without harm. I thank God for His covenant of protection, but we have to believe it and put it to work. It certainly saved my life that day.

—Julee Sherrick

Julee Sherrick is a young woman who experienced God's miraculous intervention when she called aloud for His help during a frightening personal attack right in her own home. Her parents knew about Psalm 91 and prayed its promises daily for the protection of their children, and Julee had learned the value of asserting aloud that God was her place of safety and protection. Many people would not have the courage to do it in the midst of an attack, but of all times, during a crisis is when Psalm 91 spoken out loud is most powerful. Julee, who was greatly overpowered, got out of an assault by using her mouth—not by cursing the man or threatening him, but by declaring the Word of God aloud.

YOUR *MOUTH* IS A WEAPON

God has given you Psalm 91 as a way to defend yourself with His promises, but this weapon won't do you any good if you don't know how to use it. You probably know how to use a physical weapon. If I handed you a knife, would you try to use your foot or your big toe to make it work? Of course not! That sounds ridiculous! You know to use your hands and fingers to operate physical weapons. But few people know what part of the body is used in spiritual warfare. Do you know? You operate spiritual weapons with your mouth and your tongue.

Amazingly, as insignificant as it may seem in the face of a powerful enemy, your most powerful weapon is your ability to speak the Word under pressure. In the natural Julee looked like she was unarmed, but she actually was armed with the Word of God, and it saved her from the evil intentions of this man.

SPEAK—DON'T THINK

Look closely again at verse 2 of Psalm 91—"I will say of the LORD…" (MEV). It is not enough to think it. God not only wants you to *know* that He is your refuge; He wants you to *say* it. This psalm gives you the words you need to express that you see Him as your safe place. With believing comes security, but with speaking comes authority. God wants to hear that you trust Him; merely *thinking* it is not enough to stop an attack. There is something about saying it that releases power in the unseen realm. We answer back to God what He says to us in the first verse; there is power in saying His Word back to Him. Joel 3:10 says, "Let the weak say, 'I am a mighty man.'" Circle the word *say*. Over and over we find great men of God like David, Joshua, Shadrach, Meshach, and Abednego declaring their confessions of faith aloud in dangerous situations. Notice what begins to happen on the inside when you say, "Lord, You are my refuge. You are my fortress. You are my Lord and my God. In You I put my total trust." The more we say it aloud, the more confident we become in His protection.

WATCH WHAT YOU SAY

Having two jobs is chaotic to say the least. On this particular day I got off at Doc's Pharmacy at exactly the same time I had to be at Chick-fil-A! As I drove across town, I was thinking aloud to myself, "I'm going to be late, and they're just going to

have to deal with it, because I don't get off till five and I'm supposed to be there at five!" I was going a little bit faster than I should have been because I was in a hurry, trying to get to work. To make it worse, I was driving and trying to change uniforms at the same time. *That's not a good idea. You shouldn't try it.*

Suddenly, someone a couple of cars in front of me had randomly decided to slow way, way down and make a right turn into some parking lot. Each car behind that person had to take drastic action to stop in time. The driver in front of me slammed on the brakes. Then I slammed on my brakes, pushing the pedal into the carpet. I felt my car begin to skid. I was about to wreck. In desperation I cussed out loud three times in a row. I knew I shouldn't have, but the words slipped out anyway. My life didn't pass before me, but suddenly a memory flooded my mind, reminding me of something that happened to a friend of mine…

Several years ago one of my friends was traveling in a car with some companions when a semi-truck swerved into their lane. Right before the head-on collision, they screamed, and instead of cussing, all four yelled, "Jesus!" and instantly closed their eyes. To their surprise the semi had completely missed them and was in a ditch directly behind them. No one had been hurt.

But I hadn't screamed Jesus' name; I'd said a cuss word, and as it was coming out of my mouth I was thinking, "I'm going to have a wreck. I'm going to get in a collision, and my car's going to be totaled." Then it was like the Lord reminded me, "That word is not going to do you any good, Rachel." That word doesn't have any power whatsoever; it can even have the opposite effect.

Right then I decided I was going to say, "Jesus!" three times in a row. "Jesus! Jesus! Jesus!" Then I said, "I'm sorry and I repent." And when I said that, my car stopped just in time. I had been skidding on the street and then, all of a sudden, I stopped. Unexplainably stopped—when there was no way to avoid the wreck. I was so scared I started shaking. But I was OK. No wreck, no injuries—nothing. Jesus protected me even when I had just messed up.

—Rachel Terry

Many people believe words are benign and have no real power to them. Yet if you will say aloud to yourself, "I trust You, God," you will feel a surge of confidence. On the contrary, if you say aloud to yourself, "Nothing ever works for me," then you will feel your confidence lag. Speaking your trust out loud is one of the best ways you can bolster your confidence.

When you speak God's Word to your problems, you are not convincing God; *you are convincing yourself.* You are inviting God's Word to jump off the page and come to pass for you personally. God's Word is true 100 percent of the time. In Proverbs 18:21 we read, "Death and life are in the power of the tongue" (MEV). Speak life.

There is power in saying God's Word back to Him. Start making *declarations* over your day with Bible verses. Two kinds of declarations are those using the "I am" verses, which tell us who we are in Christ, and verses declaring that we are to "fear not." Some examples include:

"I am fearfully and wonderfully made" (Ps. 139:14).

"I am forgiven" (Col. 1:14).

"I am filled with the divine nature of Christ" (2 Pet. 1:4).

"I am precious to God" (Is. 43:4).

"I am more than a conqueror through Christ" (Rom. 8:37).

"I am loved dearly by God" (John 15:13; 16:27; Rom. 5:8; Eph. 3:17-19).

"I do not fear, for You are with me. I will not be dismayed, for You are my God" (Is. 41:10).

"I will not be anxious about anything, but in everything, by prayer and petition, with thanksgiving, I will present my requests to God" (Phil. 4:6).

"I cast all my cares on You for You care for me" (1 Pet. 5:7).

"You have not given me a spirit of fear, but one of power, love, and sound mind" (2 Tim. 1:7).

"Though I walk through the valley of the shadow of death, I will fear no evil, for You are with me; Your rod and your staff, they comfort me" (Ps. 23:4).

"In my distress I prayed to You, and You answered me and set me free. You are for me, so I will have no fear. What can mere people do to me?" (Ps. 118:5–6).

Speaking your trust out loud is very important. When I am facing a challenge, I have learned to say: "In this situation [name the situation], I choose to trust You, Lord!" The difference it makes when I proclaim my trust out loud is altogether amazing.

CHAPTER 2—JOURNAL

This chapter underscored the power of declaring your trust in God and in His protection out loud. How can you begin to declare your trust in God out loud?

By Saying I Trust
You JESUS before I enter
a room and when I
wake up By saying " You
have not given me a
spirit of fear, but one of
power, love, and sound Mind
(2 Tim. 1:7

"I can do all things
through Christ who stengthen
me" (Phil 4:13)

NO MORE TRAPS

*Surely He shall deliver you from the snare of the hunter
[trapper] and from the deadly pestilence.*

—PSALM 91:3, MEV

HAVE YOU EVER seen on TV a trapper hide a big steel trap under leaves to try to catch an animal? As soon as the animal steps into the trap, it snaps shut and the animal is caught. Did you know that the enemy also has traps set for each one of us? They are not steel traps like animal trappers use. Satan uses *spiritual* traps. Spiritual traps come in many shapes and sizes, as Samantha discovered.

MOM WILL NEVER KNOW

My phone had died while I was texting with a friend. Not wanting to make her think I had started ignoring her messages, I quickly plugged the phone into the charger by my bed. When the phone turned on, I noticed that in the top corner it said the 4G was turned on. "Huh, that's weird," I thought, recollecting that the Internet privileges on my phone had been taken away. I had been grounded by my dad for using the whole family's data supply for the month all for myself. Also, I had not been honest with my parents when I was first caught.

When I realized my data privileges were turned on, I immediately sent my mom a text saying that the 4G had come on for some reason. I thought little of it and continued my conversation with my friend. A few minutes later a reply came from my mom saying that she would turn it off again. I continued my conversation for a little while longer, and then it fizzled out.

Later that night, around two o'clock, I was suddenly awake and unable to get back to sleep. I turned over looking for a comfortable position and saw my phone sitting in its usual place on the nightstand next to my bed. "No," I thought. "Remember how much trouble you've already gotten yourself into with that stupid iPhone." I closed my eyes and tried to go back to sleep, but a voice somewhere in the back of my mind just kept saying stuff like, "Come on, your mom will never know." And "It's not that big of a deal." And "Aren't you the least bit curious to see if she even turned it off?"

After five minutes I gave in and decided that I would only look at Memes on the Internet for ten minutes. Well, that ten minutes turned into an hour and ten minutes. I stared at the time, astounded at how long I had been on my phone.

"She's definitely going to notice that when she checks our data plan," I said to myself as I lay in bed staring at the ceiling. My stomach slowly worked itself into a tight knot, and I felt as if I might upchuck my fajitas. I began to tear myself up on the inside, thinking about how my mom must have had at least a little bit of trust in me since she hadn't immediately turned the data off. That thought launched me into a spiral of self-pity as I started thinking about how utterly stupid I had been. And the voice that had convinced me to use my phone was now using my actions to wreak havoc on my emotions.

I decided I would come up with a solution the following morning and went to sleep feeling stupid, unforgivable, deceptive, and pitiful all at the same time. I awoke at about eight thirty, and after remembering what had happened, I sighed and got myself a cup of coffee. Then, sitting on my bed, I began thinking of what to do. I picked up a borrowed copy of Joyce Meyer's book *Battlefield of the Mind* and started where I had left off, hoping I would find something that would help me figure out how to get out of the situation. I didn't. When I saw my mom at breakfast, the knot in my stomach grew tighter. I felt horrible knowing that she loved me and I had done the exact thing I had been told not to do. That was why I couldn't bring myself to tell her what I had done, even though that was my best option.

Later I went outside and sat on my swing. I wanted to listen to a certain song that I didn't have downloaded, so for reasons that I don't remember but I'm pretty sure weren't smart at all, I looked up the song on YouTube, using even more 4G. I didn't stop after one song and my data usage just spiraled out of control. It was then I came to the grim realization that it wasn't a matter of if I got caught; it was a matter of when. Not five minutes later my mom came outside and told me to come inside because she needed to talk to me, and I knew that I had been caught. I relayed my actions to her, and she was not pleased. She sent me to my room to finish reading *Battlefield of the Mind*.

As I sat on my bed with the book in my hand, I felt unforgivable. I asked God, "Why can't I control myself? I feel so powerless. What should I do?" He brought to my mind a Bible study that Angie [Schum] had taught one Tuesday night that was titled "You Can't Be Delivered From Your Friends."

"Samantha," God said to me, "the reason you can't let go is because deep down, even though you may not realize it, you don't want to let go and you're afraid of what might happen if you do. But you need to trust that I won't let anything hurt you. I love you and I will forgive you, but first you need to forgive yourself."

Coming to that realization made me feel much better. I knew God loved me and would never leave me even though I had fallen for one of the devil's schemes. I knew God was going to help me out of it.

—SAMANTHA, AGE 14

WHERE ARE YOU TRAPPED?

Can you think of anything in your life that could trap you subtly, much like the frog in a pan that is warmed up slowly until he eventually finds himself cooking? What could have the power to destroy your life, something you fall for time and time again? Don't be ignorant of satan's schemes, because if you are, he will take advantage of you (2 Cor. 2:11)

God warns us about this trapper, Satan. He carefully

baits his traps to appeal to each individual's weaknesses. The previous chapter focused on overcoming an outward assault (Julee's physical attack), but this chapter looks at the ways our flesh can be attacked inwardly (Samantha's internal struggle with temptation).

MANAGING FREEDOMS

When you were a child, maybe the biggest trap you faced was getting through the grocery checkout line without begging for all the candy the store put at eye level and within reach. As we mature, however, we have more freedoms to manage. Samantha's parents gave her freedom to use the data plan on the family's cell phones, and she didn't manage that freedom well. It's clear Samantha became painfully aware that she had violated the trust her parents placed in her by her statement, "I began to tear myself up on the inside, thinking about how my mom must have had at least a little bit of trust in me since she hadn't immediately turned the data off."

Life is a process of learning to manage your freedoms at each stage of life. A five-year-old isn't allowed the car keys. As you prove you can handle one level of responsibility, more and more is given to you, and consequently you are given more and more freedom.

Many college freshmen who excelled academically in high school fail their first semester in college because they have so much new freedom. They suddenly can choose to sleep in and skip class without their parents there to scold them.

The first war a college freshman has to fight is with his alarm clock and his bed. Sometimes it takes a year for students to build up their spiritual muscles enough to overcome their fleshly desire to sleep in rather than go to class. And this is where managing your freedom intersects with baited traps.

What appeals to your flesh? Doing the right thing appeals to us, but the thing our flesh desires appeals to us more (Rom. 7:18). Say hello to the trap! The flesh itself is a trap. As soon as you reach a new level of freedom, you find yourself at war with your flesh. But you may not realize what you're fighting, because up until this time others have been helping you manage your freedom and do what is right. We must learn to discipline ourselves to choose the right thing, even when our flesh wants something else. That is how we avoid Satan's traps.

The Enemy Is Real

To complicate matters, the enemy, Satan, will target you. So the problem is bigger than just having weak flesh and a lot of freedom. You have an opponent who wants to bring you down. He will try to ensnare you in some form of bondage so that you lose the freedom you have been given. And so the promise in Psalm 91:3 that God will deliver us from traps is very important.

The importance of this promise is often overlooked when people study the promises of Psalm 91. Perhaps because of the way it is written, it just seems too poetic to be applicable. But understanding this promise will help you evade the snares Satan sets for you.

THE ENEMY'S TRAPS

So often, teens are not aware that the opposition they are experiencing is actually coming from the enemy. It's easy to think everything is the result of natural causes. But 1 Peter 5:8 stresses that "the devil walks around as a roaring lion, seeking whom he may devour" (MEV).

The King James Version calls this attempt on our life "the snare of the fowler" (Ps. 91:3). This description makes me think of a net thrown by a bird catcher. You feel like you are flying high, and then a net is thrown over you, pulling you from the sky. That's what happens when you are snared.

Have you ever been emotionally soaring when suddenly something knocked you back down to earth and you crashed and burned? That is the snare of the fowler. Like the person who catches birds with a net, one thought can pull you down.

The enemy's methods are subtle and insidious. For instance, the devil loves to use depression; so many people just put up with the misery because they think it's normal. You may feel insecure and rejected and then find with every situation you get into, you end up getting deeply hurt. Someone is constantly hurting your feelings, or something is always going wrong. You fear failure, or anger is always lurking just below the surface, ready to gush out. These are tailor-made traps intentionally set for you by your enemy.

Think about your temptations. Are you being ensnared? Don't be ignorant of Satan's schemes, because if you are, he will take advantage of you.

CHAPTER 3—JOURNAL

This chapter examines the traps in life that try to ensnare us. What are some areas of weakness for you? Has the enemy ever tried to use these to trap you?

_____

_____

_____

_____

_____

_____

_____

_____

_____

_____

_____

_____

_____

NO MORE FEAR OF SICKNESS

*Surely He shall deliver you from the snare of the hunter
[trapper] and from the deadly pestilence.*

—PSALM 91:3, MEV

IN CHAPTER 3 we discussed the traps of temptation and sin. Not only does God deliver us from the snare laid by the trapper, but according to the last part of Psalm 91:3, *He also delivers us from the deadly pestilence.* I always thought pestilence was something that attacked crops—bugs, locusts, grasshoppers, spider mites, mildew, root rot. But after doing a word study on "pestilence," I found to my surprise that pestilence attacks people, not crops! A pestilence is a lethal disease.

UNREASONABLE FEAR

When Cathy Stewart was a very young girl, just two or three years old, anytime she had a pain she would immediately find herself becoming fearful. As a young child she once even had a panic attack because of her fear of illness.

One time the fear was so great she thought she was going to have a heart attack in the middle of the night. This fear passed to Cathy at a young age since the family always viewed "worst-case-scenario" fear as normal. In her earliest memories, Cathy was plagued with fear and bad dreams, and those attacks never let up.

By simply looking at Cathy, no one would know the battle that was going on inside. She was a cheerleader in high school, a DJ at the radio station, popular on the college campus, and married to Christian, one of the most sought-after men on campus. But the fear was so great that by the time she got married it had the potential to wreck her life.

She constantly had what she now calls *vain imaginations* (mental pictures of horrible diseases), which affected the significant events of her life. At that time, however, fear kept her from seeing all that she was losing out on. In the first years of her marriage, her fear of a brain tumor led her to undergo an MRI, which came back clear. She suffered from the fear of having the same sicknesses those close to her had, and pain would then follow. After a friend died of a blood clot, Cathy developed a fear of clots that plagued her pregnancy. She would go to bed at night unsure of whether she would wake up the next morning. Cathy started reading Psalm 91 every night to combat the fear until the pain went away.

Unchecked, the fear would have continued to escalate. But it never got that bad because she had people in her life who were speaking truth to her, and in time she began resisting fear.

Faithfully Christian prayed over her and stood on Psalm 91 through each attack, declaring that nothing could harm her. Then one day while listening to an audio teaching a friend had given her, Cathy heard how to overcome fear when the preacher said, "Face your fears and say to that fear, 'I am not afraid of you.'" At the end of the audio when the minister prayed, she felt like much of what she had struggled with as a child lifted off of her.

Cathy faced her fear and began to exercise her faith. She proclaimed, "Fear of sickness, I am not afraid of you any longer." She learned to push back the panic and fear when the enemy attacked her, and she was able to start placing her trust in God. She describes taking steps to freedom like peeling layers off an onion—it has been a progressive work. She starts by pinpointing the fear. Then she speaks her trust by verbalizing a promise from God's Word. Cathy says, "With every battle I can tell I'm getting stronger in God's Word because fear no longer paralyzes me. I can feel it lift off when I take authority over the fear."

—BASED ON AN INTERVIEW
WITH CATHY STEWART

Don't let fear in. Fear is not given by the Lord, so you should give it no place in your life. It can warp your personality and dominate your life. According to 2 Timothy 1:7, it makes you powerless, lacking in love, and undisciplined—it makes for a shaky life.

> For God has not given us the spirit of fear, but of power, and love, and self-control.
>
> —2 TIMOTHY 1:7, MEV

As a toddler, Cathy feared a heart attack when most children that age have never heard of such a thing. To have those fears at such a young age was highly unusual. When something that is not in line with God's Word runs down a generational line, it's easy for it to become normal—even though it made Cathy anything but normal. It wasn't until Cathy had a family of her own that she realized she was missing out on life by living in constant anxiety. Fear was controlling her life, and she decided to do something about it.

Cathy realized that trust has no fear attached to it, and she began to see fear for what it was. She had a moment of revelation when she saw the specialized traps Satan had been using for years to keep her bound to fear.

Once she got out on her own, Cathy could see that not everyone else around her fought these same kinds of fears. Her fears didn't make any sense. Why would she continually think about getting diseases? She began to realize this was an irrational way of thinking. People don't catch life-threatening diseases every day of the week, which makes you wonder, why did the devil use this trap with her?

Cathy was a worrier, so let's use worry as an illustration. What makes a person keep returning to the enemy's bait? Could it be that pride is the reason some people worry so much? People rarely think of worry as a form of pride, yet it can be. When people worry, they can tell themselves they do it because they care more than most. Worry gives you a false sense of security.

Could it be that people feel if they don't worry enough, they will let something bad into their lives? Many people think that if they don't worry intensely over those they love, they must not really care about them. To start on the road to freedom, they need to realize this is a specialized trap from which they can be set free when they understand that perfect love casts out fear (1 John 4:18).

The question you have to ask yourself is, "For what purpose is the devil using a particular trap, and why does it work on me?" Please stop and ask yourself this question right now. Get someone to help you if you need it. No matter what area you struggle with, you can be free from what has always been a trap for you in the past.

When Satan tempts you to sin, even that temptation can become a trap used to ensnare you. You must learn to heed God's warnings about hidden traps that are lying in wait for you. Remember that these are *individualized* traps—they are baited with the thing that would most likely tempt you. If you fall for the temptation and sin, it's like an animal getting caught in the trapper's snare, and it opens the door to bad things happening.

In the margin of your Bible make a note that Psalm 91:3 has two distinct parts. It mentions not only that God protects us from the trapper's snare, but also that He rescues us from *deadly pestilence* (disease). Think for a moment about the many diseases that are tormenting our world today—cancer, heart disease, diabetes, leukemia, Ebola, AIDS, and others. Is there a certain disease you fear? The world may laugh at you for believing God, but He promises to protect you from those things.

SAYING *NO*

Satan can be so clever with his traps. He uses specialized bait—bait that appeals to you. Temptation sets you up—it doesn't act like random chance. It makes sure to leave something you want unguarded so that no one will see you take it. The illusion is that you won't have to pay for what you do wrong = a world with no consequences The enemy loves to give us chances to steal, lie, cheat, or fall into whatever sin is most tempting to us individually, just to see if we'll take the bait.

The world is full of traps, and that's why God built freedom from snares into His promise of protection. It takes courage to do it right, but God will give you the strength to say *no* every time you are tempted, if you ask Him. When you fall into temptation, it shows a lack of spiritual muscle. You must build your spiritual muscles so you don't stay a weakling in an area. That strength, the power to say *no*, is one of the ways He promises to protect us, but He won't make the call on your behalf. You have to reach for His strength and decide for yourself.

If having the strength to say *no* is an area of weakness in your life, try writing this scripture on a small card: "I can do all things because of Christ who strengthens me" (Phil. 4:13, MEV). Carry it in your pocket, and pull it out and read it often. The Word of God is a real weapon, a *spiritual* weapon, and when you say it out loud and mean it, temptations retreat.

The following passage from 2 Corinthians reminds us that most battles start in our minds. Winning the battle that is going on in your thought life is crucial!

> For though we walk in the flesh, we do not war according to the flesh. For the weapons of our warfare are not carnal, but mighty through God to the pulling down of strongholds, *casting down imaginations* and

every high thing that exalts itself against the knowledge of God, bringing every thought into captivity to the obedience of Christ.

—2 CORINTHIANS 10:3–5, MEV,
EMPHASIS ADDED

Psalm 91:3 promises protection from traps. They take the form of *temptation*s that lure you into sin and imaginations that make your mind run wild. Like literal traps, they are sent *to harm you physically.* It is up to you to believe and declare God's promise to help you overcome both types of snares.

CHAPTER 4—JOURNAL

This chapter stresses the importance of recognizing the enemy's traps. What kind of bait are you most vulnerable to? What can you do to avoid Satan's traps when you encounter them?

_____

_____

_____

_____

_____

_____

_____

_____

_____

_____

_____

THE PROMISES OF GOD ARE NOT AUTOMATIC

He shall cover you with His feathers, and under His wings you shall find protection.

—P<small>SALM</small> 91:4, <small>MEV</small>

T<small>HROWN</small> O<small>UT</small> <small>OF THE</small> N<small>EST</small>

"Kalari, it is time to grow up. I won't always be there," Mom said as she dropped me off on my first day of college. "You need to develop your own prayer life…" This was the first step of jumping off the edge of the Grand Canyon into the depths of owning my own walk with God.

Mom had just lost her job, but as a single parent, she was not going to let that affect my dream of going to college. Mom made a desperate, bold move by dropping me off at college without a car, money, job, or connections and with $1,500 left to pay in tuition for room and board. Mother proclaimed, "Kalari, you're just gonna have to trust God!" Either Mom was hearing the Lord and He would come through, or I was going to be stuck six hours from home for a while. I was thrown in the deep end of the pool, and it was now sink or swim as I walked toward my first day of college.

I suddenly realized that Mom could hear God but I hadn't learned to. With growing clarity I knew if

God told Mom that He would provide for me, then He would.

I remembered when we came to visit Howard Payne University in the spring, and I was so afraid to leave home that I was making up every excuse not to come. However, my mother wasn't moved by my fear-driven complaints. She told me ever so sweetly on the campus lawn, "You can come home with me, go to a community college, start working a nine-to-five, struggling to make ends meet, and end up like me, or come here, get an education, and earn a living." I was presented with a faith opportunity that night that would change my life more than I knew.

This began my personal journey where I realized I didn't have any faith for myself. I only believed things because my mom believed them. When my mom said something would happen, I believed it would happen. Her faith was why things would always work out— all because she believed in the promises of God. I don't think I believed in them or even really knew about them. In our church youth group, we would talk about salvation and developing our character, but not much about the promises of God. In sending me off to college, my mom taught me the spiritual lesson of connecting a promise with my problem.

During my first weeks of college, I was tormented constantly with nightmares. I had no relationship with my dad, but I suddenly found myself dreaming about him. Waking myself up, I found that I had been crying in my sleep. I remember one vivid dream: Dad driving off with me running beside the car, trying to hang on the door. I felt such deep hurt. "Stop, Dad, stop!" I yelled, but he didn't stop. "Daddy, please!" He didn't even look at me. I didn't know that God could and wanted to heal a broken heart—especially *my* heart.

Through Christian discipleship I was able to forgive my dad, and I was set free from tormenting dreams. I didn't have to do this alone. God brought me Christian friends and led me to a Bible study group that has brought me closer to the Lord. I felt immediate freedom when some Christian friends prayed over me for healing from my past.

With the recurring dreams, I was told that when I woke from a bad dream, I should try to go back and re-dream the dream, but this time with the knowledge that the Lord is with me. It's funny, but you can take what you learn in the daytime and have peace come to your dreams at night.

Honestly I enjoy my walk with the Lord above all else. I have found out that I can have my own faith for answers to my problems. I've had so many of my prayers answered. My mother and I reminisce about that night on the lawn. She has even brought me back to that very spot, telling me, "We were right here when I told you about coming here. What did you say to me two weeks later? 'Mom, I know why I'm here!'"

Other people were dropping out of college all around me because of lack of finances. The Lord has supernaturally provided what I have needed. Currently I am a psychology major and about to graduate college. Yet the best news of all is that after eighteen years, my relationship with my father has been restored, because I believed by faith that he would come back to me. And now I realize that back then my mom was getting me to own my own faith.

—Kalari Faultry

Paid for Wearing the Uniform?

Kalari learned the vital lesson that we must take personal responsibility to stand on the Word. An important step in our maturity is learning to add our faith to the prayers that our family prays over us and not making someone else do all the work.

A sense of personal entitlement permeates our whole culture. It couldn't be more obvious than in the example of a high schooler who got his first job and found out he was actually expected to work. He decided to quit when he was asked to do something he didn't *feel* like doing. When he was questioned about what he had done to deserve a paycheck, all he could come up with was that he had put on the company uniform.

It's hard to believe this is actually a true story, but tragically, we often think this way in our walk with God. Too many times we "put on the uniform" and think that just because we're a Christian God's promises are automatic. The modernized story of David fighting Goliath has become "David waiting around for God to strike Goliath with a lightning bolt." Giving our bare minimum is an entitlement idea. It's like assuming the uniform is enough. What does the Bible say we should "do" as Christians? David had to "do" something. The secret is finding what God would have us do in order to connect to the promises.

HAWKS, CHICKS, AND HENS

God gave me an illustration of this that I will never forget. Often He gives us an example in nature so we can better understand His Word. This one played out right before my eyes, and I was shocked at what I witnessed...

> My husband and I live in the country, and one spring our old mother hen hatched some baby chicks. One afternoon, when the little chicks were scattered all over the yard, I suddenly saw the shadow of a hawk overhead. What happened next taught me a lesson I will never forget. What I thought would happen and what did happen were two different things. The mother hen did not run all over the barnyard and jump on top of those chicks in an attempt to cover them with her wings as one might have expected. I thought the old hen would pick her favorite chicks in a split second and run to cover them. No!
>
> Instead, to my surprise, she squatted down, spread out her wings, and began to squawk. Without hesitation, those little chicks came running to her from every direction and then ducked under those outstretched wings. All the mother hen did was cluck and expand her wings so her chicks knew where to hide. Then she pulled her wings down tight, tucking every little chick safely under her. There was no way the hawk could get to those babies without going through the mother hen.
>
> When I think of those baby chicks running to

their mother, I'm reminded that we have to run to God. He doesn't run all over the place trying to put His covering over us. He says, "I have made protection available. You run to Me!" If one of those chicks had tried to hide itself or failed to heed its mother's warning clucks, it would have been snatched up by the hawk. And when we run to God in faith, it means the enemy has to go through God to get to us. There is no greater safety. "Under His wings" is a very inviting place. Knowing that God's refuge is described as a literal wing thrown over us should make us feel exceedingly safe and protected.

—Peggy Joyce Ruth

What Part Do *You* Play?

Jerusalem, Jerusalem, who kills the prophets and stones those who are sent to her! How often I wanted to gather your children together, the way a hen gathers her chicks under her wings, and you were unwilling.

—Matthew 23:37

It would be hard to miss the contrast between God's willingness and our unwillingness—His "wanting" against our "not wanting," His "would" against our "would not." Is He offering us something we don't accept? This verse from Matthew describes what it looks like to shun the protection of the wing.

Do we play a part in our relationship with the Lord? I've always wondered what would have happened on the first Passover if the Israelites hadn't stayed under the blood (Exod. 12:13). The Bible doesn't make an example out of anyone who didn't come in under the protection of the blood for us to know the answer for sure, but it does indicate that the protection was only available to those in the right location that night, *under the blood.*

And that is the point—we have to make an effort to be *under the wing,* next to the most intimate part, the beating warm heart. The protection of the wing is not automatic. Ask yourself, "Will I do my part to seek refuge under God's upraised wing?" So many people come to Christianity thinking God has to do everything for them, and that is a misconception. People have asked, "So-and-so was a Christian—why didn't Psalm 91 work for him?" To put it as bluntly as possible: We don't come into the world with Psalm 91 (or any other promise for that matter) tattooed on our backside. It is available, but it is not automatic.

Only one thief looked at Jesus and asked, "Remember me!" (See Luke 23:32–43.) Jesus died for both thieves, but it didn't do one of them any good because he didn't "do" his part and accept the offer Jesus had made for both of them. We have to answer with our hearts and our mouths (Rom. 10:9–10). Like the thief on the cross, we can be next to Jesus and miss Him!

Too many people see Psalm 91 as a great promise that they file right alongside all the other books their mom gave them to read. But it will be too late for those who never pray the psalm and wait until something bad happens to try to find God's outstretched wing. For instance, Joe Teenager watches TV and plays video games regularly but never gets into his hiding place to spend time with God, and then—*bam!*—trouble strikes. Then he remembers Psalm 91 and those great promises of protection!

We tend to use Psalm 91 as medicine after we are sick, instead of as vitamins to prevent sickness. It's like frantically brushing your teeth after the dentist tells you your mouth is full of cavities. To use another analogy, the *best* time to pray Psalm 91 is not as you lie on a stretcher coming off the football field with an injury, but in the locker room before the game.

So how can you put Psalm 91 into action before trouble strikes? One way to hide under God's wing is to say and believe: "Lord, I choose to hide under Your wings of protection. I choose not to rely on my own strength to get through this, but I trust in You and Your Word in this situation."

Young people need to know that they have a responsibility in obtaining God's safety. The young chick has a choice to go under the wing or not, to try to hide himself from danger or totally ignore what God is offering. Kalari, the boy in his uniform, David the warrior, and *you* have to do something to receive the promises. Just because Psalm 91 is in your Bible doesn't make it your experience. Each person has a part to play in his or her own protection.

CHAPTER 5—JOURNAL

This chapter is a reminder that our protection is not automatically just because we are Christians. This chapter is special to me because of the illustration from my own backyard. The story of the hen clucking and raising her wings so the chicks could run for protection from the hawk sticks with you when you realize you have a part to play in getting to safety. What can you do to put Psalm 91 into practice *before* trouble strikes?

_____

_____

_____

_____

_____

_____

_____

_____

_____

Chapter 6

BEHIND HIS SHIELD

His faithfulness shall be your shield and wall.

—PSALM 91:4, MEV

GOD HAS PROVIDED a shield to cover you, and that shield is God Himself. Your faith in His promises and in His faithfulness to do what He says He will do activates His shield around you to protect you from danger.

My son, Bill, played football in school, and we prayed Psalm 91 over him the entire time he played through his senior year. He was always a little afraid that we might come down from the stands and pray over him right on the fifty yard line, so Bill said he prayed Psalm 91 himself so his *mother* would stay seated.

Whatever you do in life, this promise of a shield is invaluable for your prayer life. Here's another family's football experience with Psalm 91.

SPORTS HELMETS AND SHIELDS

 My family knew the power of Psalm 91 and claimed its promises for the whole family but especially me since I was very active and played football from grade school through college. We stood firm praying the psalm over me for no injuries. I

remember being in a tough game one night and my foot rolling over onto my ankle. I actually heard it pop. I thought, "Oh, man!" as I limped to the side line. I sat down on the bench and a trainer looked at my ankle. I began to pray for God to heal my ankle. After the trainer finished looking it over, I told him it felt fine and hopped up and went back in the game. And I never had trouble with it again.

The closest I ever came to a serious injury was my freshman year of high school. On this particular play I was playing fullback. The quarterback handed me the football and I ran a drive up the middle. On this play, however, I did something you should never do when running the football—I put my head down. As I collided with the other players, their pads hit the back of my helmet, pushing my head to the ground.

The injury was extremely painful and looked like it could be very serious. The doctor said I had strained all the muscles in my neck and there was nothing he could do to treat it. He even recommended that I stop playing, but that was never going to happen. This is when my parents discovered a chiropractor to help get my neck back in shape to play football. I never stopped playing football, and for the next seven years I played on into college.

I know God protected me from a serious spine and neck injury even though I did something stupid. It's quite a testimony when you think about it: God has protected me in every sport I've played, especially in the sometimes violent sport of football. I never broke a bone, had a life-altering injury, or even missed a game in those eleven years. Praying God's Psalm 91 protection was a staple to me playing sports. Praying Psalm 91 protection became the norm for my family, and I pray it will become normal for you as well.

—Christian McDaniel

Your Faith + His Faithfulness

Imagine a shield, a proper one, fashioned from the thickest steel, so big you can hide yourself behind it and not be seen at all. God is that kind of shield. *Your faith in His promises and in His faithfulness in keeping them becomes a shield*, and this shield will encircle you to protect you from whatever tries to come against you. When the devil tells you that you are not good enough, realize *God's* goodness is your shield. Use the shield of His faithfulness to push back against every unfaithful thing in your life.

Let's think about this. Just because we have a part to play doesn't mean the protection depends on us. Our effort is very small, just like the effort to get behind a shield; all we have to do is get behind God and His promises. And like a shield, He is stronger than any armor. What a wonderful truth that our protection begins and ends with Him: He promises it. He fulfills it.

Many times we think of a shield that is just in front of us. A frontal shield is a good thing to have, but this shield is different. The Hebrew word for shield (*tsinnah*) in Psalm 91:4 is very unusual in that this particular shield goes all the way around the person. The Hebrew word for buckler or fortress, *cocherah*, is even more unique; it is used only once in the entire Bible and is not found in other writings. It also means something surrounding the person and carries the idea of being both cold and prickly. It could imply a 3-D effect or a sort of bubble of protection. Sometimes it is translated "the surrounding of a fortress of safety or armor." This multifaceted concept of protection has deep meaning. But the bottom line is this: God's shield of protection encompasses a person on all sides.

Some people live insecure, fearful lives because they never realize they are covered by a shield. You gain confidence when you recognize that you are covered with invisible protection that stands between you and evil. Soldiers tell very interesting stories about this supernatural occurrence. We will share two *old stories* here, but let's give them *new meaning* because they will help you understand the shield over your life.

We were on a tour of Mount Vernon when we heard this story:

> A young man in his early twenties would become a legend on the battlefields of the French and Indian War. In 1755, General Braddock was leading 1,300 soldiers into battle with the French and Indians, and one officer in particular would rise above the ranks of what is possible with man. While marching to overtake a fort in the north, General Braddock's troops were ambushed by the French and Indians. They were surrounded, being shot at from both sides. The general's troops were poorly equipped for this type

of *warfare*, only being trained to fight an enemy standing directly in front of them.

The French and Indians were hidden in the trees and brush surrounding them, making the 1,300 soldiers sitting ducks. Despite these terrible odds, one officer would rise above the seemingly hopeless situation. The battle lasted a mere two hours, but 714 of the 1,300 soldiers were killed or wounded, and eighty-five of the eighty-six officers on horseback were taken to the ground. Only one officer remained unharmed. His name was George Washington.

The future president of the United States was somehow still standing and rallied the remaining troops to retreat to their fort. The next day Washington wrote to his family, telling them that several horses were shot out from under him and that he found *four bullet holes* in his jacket (army uniforms during this time period were not loose like the jackets we wear today, but were buttoned and tightly fitted). Four holes and not a single bullet touched him! The *hand of God* was all over him. Fifteen years after the battle, Washington would meet with the Indian chief who opposed them that day. The chief told Washington how he had commanded his men to single out the officers on horseback, yet no one could hit Washington. The chief himself fired *seventeen shots* at Washington, failing each time to hit his mark. He believed George Washington was protected by the Great Spirit. In a letter, George Washington gave God credit for what happened that day in battle.

Both men could sense the *invisible shield*. Washington was so aware of it that he wrote home to tell his family about this amazing protection, and fifteen years later the chief was still stunned over this man who could not be harmed by their bullets.

And again another famous time in history when a shield was evident:

> World War II is one of history's best examples of a *shield*. During the dreadful yet heroic week in May of 1940, when the British army had been forced into total retreat and lay exposed on the sandy shores of Dunkirk, France, many miracles occurred. Lying hopelessly exposed, pinned down by Nazi planes and heavy artillery, and armed only with their rifles, the brave troops were seemingly trapped by the channel with no place to turn for protection. A British chaplain told of lying facedown in the sand for what seemed an eternity on the shell-torn beach at Dunkirk. Nazi bombers dropped their lethal charges, causing shrapnel to kick up sand all around him, while other planes repeatedly sprayed his position with their machine guns blazing. Although dazed by the explosions around him, the British chaplain suddenly became aware that, in spite of the deafening roar of the shells and bombs falling all around him, he had not been hit. With bullets still raining down about him, he stood and stared with amazement at the outline of his own shape in the sand. It was the only smooth and undisturbed spot on the entire bullet-riddled beach. His heavenly shield must have fit the exact shape of his body.[1]

Most of the time we don't need a shield to protect us from real bullets being sprayed at us, but it's good to know that this shield has been tested and proved under such conditions. George Washington's story is one of outstanding bravery; it makes no logical sense how he not only survived but was the only officer who couldn't be hit. His uniform jacket wasn't shielded, but his body was! And this chaplain on the sands of Dunkirk was crying out Psalm 91 only to have his shield proven to him as he viewed the bullet indentions in the sand. It formed the shape of his body when he had no place to hide, and he found himself under the wing of the Most High!

Christian understood Psalm 91 as providing a shield for him when he played contact sports. He and his family prayed for and believed in Psalm 91 protection over him. Soldiers also give us a good example since they need shields as part of their very job description and are often on the front lines of danger. Though sports helmets and bullet-proof vests offer limited protection, your invisible shield in the spiritual realm is the most important gear you can wear.

CHAPTER 6—JOURNAL

This chapter stresses the importance of knowing that a shield is available to us. Few people realize that part of God's nature is to be a literal shield of protection for us. Our faith in God's promises and in His faithfulness to do what He says He will do becomes a shield around us to protect us from danger. How can you remind yourself that God is your shield of protection?

_____

_____

_____

_____

_____

_____

_____

_____

_____

_____

Chapter 7

I WILL NOT FEAR TERROR

You shall not be afraid of the terror by night.

—PSALM 91:5, MEV

NIGHT VISITOR

During a college summer ses-
sion, my roommate and I were
living off campus in a small
two-bedroom house on a busy
street. One Friday night, my
roommate and other friends
from our college-age church
group decided to go to Jack and
Peggy Joyce Ruth's house in the
country to watch movies. Because I was tired and had
to work the next day, I decided to stay home.

Our house was small and cozy, with a single
attached garage and a small backyard. On a Friday
night, you could typically hear cars roaring past
on our neighborhood street. Our landlord and his
family lived next door.

As my roommate, Ceil, left the house with my
other friends, she left explicit instructions to lock the
front screen door. We had no central air and would
often let the night breezes blow in through the screen.
I let them out and locked the door as instructed,
although all the windows were open as well.

I was in my little bedroom, just feet from the

49

front door, studying God's Word. Peggy Joyce Ruth had been teaching (off and on) about Psalm 91 and God's umbrella of protection over us. I've always loved to memorize scripture and had begun memorizing Psalm 91. I loved this psalm—it was such a love letter of protection to me.

As I studied the Word, the only noises I could hear were from the street. I was surprised when I suddenly heard the front door rattle. I didn't think much of it at first, but then it became persistent, as if someone was trying to get the door to swing open. It rattled harder and harder, and then a male voice started yelling out, "Let me in, let me in! I know you're in there—let me in!"

My roommate had warned me that many weekend nights our landlord came home drunk and could be heard next door in a drunken brawl with his family. Because she'd also warned me that he had made advances toward her, I figured he had come to the door thinking she was home. I had not met him at this point since I had moved in only a couple of weeks earlier. Who knows who was at that door, but I knew I had an escalating problem on my hands.

The rattling and pulling on the door seemed to go on for ages. As I sat frozen to my bed, my first thoughts were of God's protective psalm, Psalm 91. Because it was deep in my spirit and memory, I automatically began quoting it aloud: "He that dwelleth in the secret place of the Most High shall abide under the shadow of the Almighty. I will say of the LORD, He is my refuge and my fortress: my God; in him will I trust…" and on and on. I had my Bible raised to the ceiling, and I was practically shouting Psalm 91 as I shut out the fear of the circumstance that was happening.

At some point, I crawled to the phone in Ceil's room across the way and called the Ruths' house. I whispered that someone was trying to get in the house, and would someone please come back into town. I hung up and with my Bible in one hand and the nearest stick-like weapon I could find (I think I grabbed a garden tool) in the other, I stood in the hallway, not daring to come into the dim light of the doorway, and kept yelling Psalm 91.

The loud rattling and shaking and yelling subsided.

Soon I heard Angelia Ruth's big old car racing up the drive. Although she later told me the drive had taken longer than usual because the young man driving kept killing the clutch until Angie ordered him out of the driver's seat, they arrived at just the right time.

My friends walked up to the porch, reached the screen door and as they took hold of the handle the screen door opened. The hook and eye closure of the screen door wasn't attached at all; the man's attempts to get inside must have completely loosened the latch.

These things I know: I latched the door, I heard the rattles of a latched door, and I heard the cries of a man half crazed by alcohol or evil intent. I had the presence of mind in this time of trouble to use the Word of God in Psalm 91, and I held a garden tool as a weapon. I also must have had a very large angel standing at the screen door—both when it was latched and when it became unlatched. I called down the promises of God in Psalm 91 as my umbrella of protection, and the devil *had* to flee. I resisted him and his devices, but only through the Word of God.

To this very day, Psalm 91 is on my mind when things don't seem right in the house or I am alone in an unfamiliar place with unfamiliar people. I have traveled many miles by plane and prayed Psalm 91 when a flight was having trouble. Time and time again, God has proven Himself to me and to those around me through the words of this Psalm.

I am most thankful for the teaching of the Word in my life at a young age. It has definitely endured through my life.

—JO ANN SOMERS HONEY

The fifth verse of Psalm 91 reminds us that Satan will send dangers and terrors our way, especially in the darkness of night. Young people may face all kinds of frightening situations. Just walking down a dark street late at night can cause fear.

Jo Ann faced her terror head-on and experienced firsthand the truth of Psalm 91:5: "You shall not be afraid of the terror by night, nor of the arrow that flies by day" (MEV). Notice this verse covers the entire twenty-four-hour period by emphasizing *day and night* protection. Fear in the night of the things you can't see is a natural feeling, but God is still there with you.

GOD ALREADY HAS A PLAN FOR EVERY EVIL THING

You may have noticed how Psalm 91:5–6 addresses different kinds of evil in groups in order to cover *any evil thing* that can befall you. The first group in verse 5 is described as "terror by night." Think of the kinds of crime we typically fear; this evil that God calls "terror by night" includes every terrorizing thing *another person* can do to harm you. This group includes all the evil that comes through human agency—physical assault, kidnapping, robbery, murder, terrorist attacks—as well as night terrors, which interrupt our sleep.

As surprising as it seems, fear is an unnecessary ingredient in our lives: "He shall not be afraid of evil tidings; his heart is fixed, trusting in the LORD" (Ps. 112:7, MEV). Through this verse God is saying, "Don't be afraid of what people can do to you. I will protect you." Push back with the Word against the terror that tries to seize you.

The ability to confront terror without fear is an amazing promise (even if you are waving whatever stick, club, or garden tool you can find in the other hand)!

CHAPTER 7—JOURNAL

This chapter looks at God's deliverance from all forms of terror. Many people struggle with night terrors, and we've seen how Psalm 91:5 promises deliverance from this kind of fear. This chapter also addresses the terror of what another person can do to harm us. What are some ways we can combat fear?

_____

_____

_____

_____

_____

_____

_____

_____

_____

_____

Chapter 8

I WILL NOT FEAR ARROWS

You shall not be afraid ... of the arrow that flies by day.

—PSALM 91:5, MEV

SURROUNDED ON ALL SIDES

Jake Weise remembers climbing into a black military Hummer at his base in Fallujah. Tall, blond, and powerfully built, Jake had wanted to be a US Marine for as long as he could remember. Now an infantry machine gunner and a

corporal in Golf Company, Second Battalion, First Marines, he was on his second deployment to Iraq. His duties centered in and around the city of Fallujah, a town forty miles west of Baghdad. It had been one of the most peaceful places in Iraq, but by September 24, 2004, the insurgent leader, Abu Musab al-Zarqawi, had pulled together some five thousand troops. Many of them were not Iraqis. Now Fallujah was a violent place controlled by a brutal and unpredictable enemy.

Since June, Jake and his team had held the highway on the east side of Fallujah, which linked the city with Ramadi and Baghdad. They called it the "cloverleaf," and since it was such a good transportation route, the insurgents wanted it badly. By now the terrain was rough and war-torn, but things had been quiet for several months, and Jake could almost feel hostility simmering like the sun on the desert sand in summer. He knew by now that peace in a war zone was nothing but an illusion; the quiet meant the enemy was planning their next attack.

Hearing gunfire, Jake immediately headed toward the cloverleaf. There was no question in his mind that the US soldiers were fighting for their lives. Jake was a good marine, and he stayed prepared. In battle, instinct kicked in as a result of the rigorous training he had been through. He was praying Psalm 91 by the time the Hummer had slipped into gear: "He who dwells in the shelter of the Most High…"

Arriving at the cloverleaf, Jake heard the firing, jumped out of the Hummer with his weapon drawn, and rolled behind sandbags. The men had already suffered one hit, and now the attack had reached an insane level. The insurgents had perfect cover in the tall surrounding buildings, and they were able to keep up their intense fire. Their elevated positions also allowed them to watch every move Jake and his men made. They were hemmed in, unable to budge. Minutes turned into an hour and then two while the insurgents never let up, but Jake and his marines held their position.

Jake fired, doing what he'd been trained to do, but he also prayed, again doing what he'd been trained to do. Locked in a fight for life, Jake thought back to his days in Brownwood, Texas. There, a woman named Peggy Joyce Ruth had taught the most complete breakdown of Psalm 91 that he'd ever heard.

Until then, Jake had never imagined the power locked in that psalm, so he had made a decision that day to pray the psalm over himself every day, as did his family, and he had returned home from his first deployment without a scratch. But he'd never encountered anything like what he was facing now. It was war at a pitch he'd never imagined.

After a couple of hours and over the uproar of the fight, Jake heard the most beautiful sound he'd ever heard—Cobra helicopter gunships, AC-130 Spectre gunships, and F-18 fighter jets, along with Combined Anti-Armor Teams with heavy machine guns and tube-launched, optically tracked anti-tank missiles. But before he could rejoice, one of the Cobras was shot down. He'd been praying for hours nonstop. He'd prayed (not just prayed, declared!) Psalm 91 so often for both himself and his company that now it flowed to God like his next breath.

Even with heavy support from above and on the ground, the insurgents didn't let up. "I will not fear terror by night…arrows by day…A thousand may fall at my side…"

Hours of unrelenting fire later, a sniper hit Jake's company commander. It was a clean shot to the head. The bullet didn't penetrate the bone. Instead, it followed the arc of his skull, leaving a nasty gash along his scalp.

Sniper fire also hit another marine in the head, but again, the bullet didn't penetrate the man's skull.

After almost seven hours of unrelenting fire, the tanks and other heavy support weapons started leveling the buildings close to Jake and his team's forward fighting holes. With that, the fire let up.

Determined to take the cloverleaf, the insurgents regrouped and attacked again the following day. Furious, intense fire rained down on them, but again Jake and his team drove them back.

Over the next week, the battled raged. One marine took a hit in the right knee. The bullet went under the kneecap and between the bones, leaving a clean penetration.

A 50-caliber bullet hit another marine in the armpit, where it punctured his lung and lodged in his sternum. "You can't call surviving a 50-caliber slug anything except miraculous," Jake says. "And what are the chances of two head shots that didn't penetrate the bone? The bullets were supposed to explode on impact."

Jake said that he prayed and stood on Psalm 91 during all those battles and never felt so much as a piece of shrapnel pass by him. Despite weeks and weeks of firefights, Jake's company didn't have a single man killed in action in June, July, August, or September. Jake knew that had to be a direct result of prayer covering him and his company. When he got home, he told how he witnessed miracles from the hand of God simply by believing and standing on the Word of God in Psalm 91.

Jake Weise and the Golf Company not only survived the attack; they protected the cloverleaf from falling into the hands of the insurgents. In the history of the war in Iraq, September 24, 2004, will be forever remembered. The massive insurgent attacks that day sparked the Second Battle of Fallujah, waged in November and December.

Jake completed his tour of duty in Iraq without a single injury—spirit, soul, or body. When he left Iraq, he didn't leave behind his faith. Wherever he goes, he is a marine, but more than that, he is a man who walks in the awareness of his divine protection.

—BASED ON AN INTERVIEW WITH JAKE WEISE

Although the US military puts gear on our soldiers to protect them, Jake was in more armor than could be seen by the natural eye—the Lord was the defense of his life against every bullet being fired at him. And as good as his gear was, he needed more. Jake told us he could actually feel the words of Psalm 91 pumping through him. Jake faced bullets not arrows as Psalm 91:5 mentions, but the intent of an enemy is the same—to aim at the spot that will take the opponent out.

How the Enemy Attacks

An arrowhead is relatively small, but it is made to strike with precision. Arrows are not fired at random but are meticulously and skillfully aimed to strike the weakest and most vulnerable points. Consequently, knowing you are under attack is half the battle.

Look at the thoughts that always return to you. Consider the repeated feelings of depression, rejection, isolation, insecurity, anxiety—anything that keeps coming back to attack you again and again. Satan is smart enough to stick with what works, and unless you're protected, his arrows will find their mark. Some arrows are sent to hurt you physically, while others may be emotional or spiritual. Remember, arrows are sent deliberately and are aimed maliciously at the spot that will cause the most damage.

Satan's arrows are targeted toward those areas where our minds are not renewed by the Word of God. Perhaps an arrow is directed toward where we are still losing our temper, or where we are easily offended, or where we feel rebellious or fearful.

Another kind of arrow is a difficulty or a problem sent to disrupt your life. People often don't realize that the "steal, kill, destroy" problems they face are actually arrows sent by the enemy (John 10:10).

Think about the areas where you feel the most weakness, and you will know where to expect the most vicious attacks. It's not fair; in fact, it's cruel, but this is how Satan works—he will aim his attack at the place you are most vulnerable. Remember that "no weapon that is formed against you shall prosper" (Isa. 54:17, MEV). Arrows are weapons like any other, and they can be struck down and outclassed. The Word of God is the strongest spiritual weapon in existence, and it can destroy any arrow sent against you.

What are the vulnerable areas in your life? Where do attacks happen over and over? Where have problems become a repeating cycle in your life?

The Lord would not have made this promise to protect you from the arrows of the enemy if He had not intended for you to believe Him and claim victory. Though arrows may fly through the air toward you (Eph. 6:16), they don't have to hit their mark. People often give up when the arrow has been released straight for their head or heart. They don't run to God's wing for shelter, or they drop their shield of faith and *let* the arrow hit its mark. We must take a different tactic. This is the time to resist and stand firm.

CHAPTER 8—JOURNAL

This chapter explores God's deliverance from arrows targeted toward those areas that will hurt us the most. Satan fires arrows deliberately with the intention of wounding us. Where do attacks happen over and over in your life? How can you block those arrows before they strike?

_____

_____

_____

_____

_____

_____

_____

_____

_____

_____

_____

I WILL NOT FEAR PESTILENCE

You will not be afraid . . . of the pestilence that stalks in darkness.

—PSALM 91:5–6

HAVING YOUR OWN FAITH

While I was at Howard Payne University in Brownwood, Texas, the pain in my abdomen became so intense I passed out during a voice lesson.

Before I left home, my dad was outnumbered with three teenage girls in his brood. But he didn't mind. He said he was spoiled having that many women to look after him, but he spoiled us as well.

In my teen years I struggled with intense pain during my monthly cycle. The cramps were so severe I was often bedridden for two or three days a month. Yet Mom faithfully prayed me through them. Unfortunately, when I went off to college, the pain began to intensify. I remember regularly calling my mom for prayer. "Of course I'll pray for you," she told me. "But now that you're off to college, you need to develop your *own* faith muscles. You pray, and I'll agree."

I had let my mom pray for me—for everything— all of my life. At this time, I was just enjoying the relatively carefree life of being a college student and wasn't too vigilant about my faith, but I knew my mother was! Mom was like a rock.

At the age of twenty a doctor's diagnosed me with endometriosis. The debilitating cramps that I'd had all my growing-up years continued to occur on a monthly basis, and I was fearful of the potential infertility due to the scarring left by each episode.

Then one year later, I lay on the floor out cold.

On the way to the ground I had hit my head on the piano. When I regained consciousness with the aid of water and paper towels from my vocal coach, I called my parents. My father came and rushed me back home to Midland, Texas. As I walked in the back door of my parents' home, I was met by my mother. She boldly stated, "We can do this two ways—God's way or man's way. Which is it going to be?"

Through tears, I decided to do it God's way. I prayed as my mom laid hands on me and spoke the promises of God's Word over me in the name of Jesus. And I received it! We believed by faith that I was healed.

Since that day, I have never even had cramps. My husband, Kevin, and I have four children, two of whom were complete surprises.

During an exam after I had been healed, I asked my gynecologist if there was any scarring due to endometriosis. There was none. His comment was, "There's no way you've had endometriosis." God healed me so completely that there wasn't even a remnant of that disease, and my fears of infertility were proven wrong in an abundant and beautiful way.

Kevin, like my dad, was surrounded by three girls who spoil him. However, we have had a new arrival—a baby boy. Since that day I passed out at voice lessons, my faith has grown. I am no longer that college student who had to be rushed home for my mom to pray. In my growing-up years, my parents were the strong ones, but I learned from them to run directly to God.

—RACHEL DULIN KOONTZ

"Why, God? Why would You allow this to happen to me?" We often ask this question when we face pain. Psalm 91 addresses even the most extreme things we might face, and it gives us many promises.

GOD DOES NOT WASTE WORDS

Since God doesn't waste words, He must have a specific reason for repeating His promise that we will not fear pestilence. When people say something more than once, they are usually trying to emphasize a point. God knew that pestilence and fear would run rampant during the days we are living in. The world is teeming with fatal epidemics that are hitting people by the thousands.

Sometimes we have trouble believing these promises in Psalm 91 because we are surrounded by people who don't believe God's Word. That's why we need to change our thinking until it lines up with the way God sees things. So many people think it's normal to be sick. Truthfully, sickness is not a natural state of being. But God goes even beyond that. He has put something in each of our bodies that makes it attempt to heal itself. For example, if someone has a cut on the finger, it closes back up. And the body works hard to rid itself of toxins, poisons, infections, etc.

Doctors rely heavily on the body's ability to heal itself. God put this capacity for healing within our very design, and He reinforces His promise to protect us from pestilence by stating it twice, in verses 3 and 5–6. It is important to use not only our natural tools but also the scriptural promises God has given.

As we grow from child to adult, we assume more responsibility for ourselves. We can see this progression in the natural order of things—we feed ourselves, we clean up when we make a mess, we earn a living, we take care of those we are responsible for—but we cannot forget that spiritually we also grow in responsibility for ourselves. We build up protection against sickness (both physical and spiritual) by knowing God's Word and claiming its promises for ourselves.

Start praying Psalm 91 when you are young. Pray *before* something attacks you. Preventative prayer is choosing to play offense rather than defense. Be proactive in developing your faith muscles.

FAITH IS A CHOICE

Some people think faith is hard, but that's because they think faith is a *feeling*. Faith is not a feeling, but a choice. Faith is simply *choosing* to believe what God says in His Word and refusing to doubt. We can have faith in the preventative stage, when things are going well; in our present circumstances, even if we may be going through something difficult; and even in the worst possible situation, when we are facing immediate defeat.

Psalm 91 is for every season and every stage of difficulty in your life. Someone has joked, "There are only two times the devil will strike you—when you are out of the will of God, and when you are in the will of God!" No matter what you are going through right now, choose faith!

What If We Miss the Preventative Stage?

Even though prevention is best, cure is available if we miss that stage. We can overcome after we have been attacked in our vulnerable spot or assaulted relentlessly. With God all things are possible, even when the world thinks it is too late and has given up.

God's Word is medicine to your whole body (Prov. 4:22). If an attack has already happened, the Word is medicine and it has the power to heal. If you are in a desperate situation, ask someone to pray over you. But if you are under heavy assault, you more than likely will have to get aggressive with the Word of God to turn the tide of the battle.

I knew a young man who compiled a list of scripture verses about healing and read them into a recorder, then played that recording over and over until it was easy for him to believe God's Word on healing. God has told you that you don't have to be afraid of diseases. So find a way that works for you to get these promises down inside you until you believe them with all your heart.

CHAPTER 9—JOURNAL

This chapter covers deliverance from pestilence and every form of fatal disease. Is it hard for you to believe God wants to heal? Why or why not? What does the Bible say about God's desire to heal?

_____

_____

_____

_____

_____

_____

_____

_____

_____

_____

_____

_____

I WILL NOT FEAR DESTRUCTION

You will not be afraid . . . of the destruction that lays waste at noon.

—PSALM 91:5–6

BACKYARD TORNADO

When my parents had me go outside and speak to a tornado, I realized I didn't have normal parents. It dawned on me that when parents put their children outside quoting God's Word in the face of a storm, they must really believe the stories in the Bible.

The radio warned us that the tornado was headed straight for our house. I could feel faith rising in my heart as my parents placed us in a position to put our faith in action. I know this seems strange, but it actually made my faith go to a higher dimension when my parents involved my brother, Bill, and me in this bold action of speaking to the storm. I *knew* they loved me. I *knew* they wanted us to be protected. I *knew* they believed what the Bible said even more than what fear was saying, and I *knew* they had set the course of action for the family that night to bring about protection.

It was quite a scene when some friends who were spending the night joined us because Mom and Dad asked us all to come out and help them pray.

We were all in our pajamas outside *praying up a storm!* Just as Jesus spoke to the storm, "Peace, be still!" we were going to speak to a storm and find out exactly how much of the Word of God had been hidden in our hearts. For the first time, I realized I didn't have Psalm 91 completely memorized. I had to repeat the words after my parents. What a faith builder it was for us when that tornado lifted back into the sky and disappeared. There were storm chasers parked out on our country road from a local React Club who were giving the local radio station minute-by-minute reports. The radio DJ quoted these weathermen as saying they had witnessed a miracle when the tornado dissipated back up into the clouds. When a tornado is headed directly for you and your home on top of a hill and you see the power of God protect you from disaster, it is one of those moments you never forget.

This story has always fascinated people. The next day when my teacher at school had us tell what we did during the tornado alarms, he totally wasn't expecting my answer. And honestly, I wanted to crawl under a desk rather than tell him what we actually did, but I couldn't deny that it had worked. While others hid in bathtubs with mattresses piled on top of them or locked themselves in closets for hours in the dorms, Mom and Dad took us to the only thing that was undeniably secure—God's Word!

—ANGELIA RUTH SCHUM

There is no place in the world where you can go to be safe from every natural disaster. Destruction can also come in the form of life-threatening accidents or events. We're not saying that to put fear in you, but to make you realize that while there is no safe place *in the world* to hide, God says you can run to His shelter and not be afraid of the destruction, because He provides a safe place in the midst of it.

Every evil known to humankind will fall into one of the four groups in Psalm 91:5–6: terror (*evil things done by others*), arrows (*temptations, attacks, and obstacles*), pestilence (*deadly diseases*), and destruction (*natural or self-inflicted disasters*). The amazing thing is that God has told you He will protect you from all of these things if you put your trust in Him.

ACTS OF WHO?

Destruction can be an evil over which people have no control, including catastrophes such as storms, floods, fires, and accidents. The world may call these things acts of God, but He is not the one trying to destroy you. When Jesus commanded the storm to cease in Mark 4:39, it became perfectly calm, showing us that God is not the one who sends natural disasters; Jesus never would have gone against His Father by rebuking something if God had sent it.

There will always be some people who won't believe God's promises of protection, even if you show them the scriptures in the Bible, but that doesn't keep the promises from being true for those who do believe. (See Romans 3:3-4 and 2 Corinthians 1:20.) Don't let anyone talk you out of this covenant; it is better to trust God than to go by what other people say.

HUMAN TORNADOES

Destruction could include many things. There are natural tornados and there are people who are like tornados. Their lives are bent on destruction, and they recklessly suck in and attempt to destroy everything in their path. We all know these kinds of people. Sometimes they will tell you to do the right thing even while they do what's wrong. Often these human tornadoes are the life of the party and seem very popular, but it's easy to see they leave many hurt people in their wake.

It's best to get out of their path of destruction and pray for them from a distance. Nonetheless, God can protect you even when you're around someone who is bent on destruction if you will cry out to Him. He has good plans for you.

DESTRUCTION

Examine John 10:10 and see how evil progresses. The thief's job description is to steal, kill, and destroy. Destruction is the enemy's ultimate goal for our lives. But Jesus has better plans; He gives us not only life, but life more abundantly. And you can see the progression in this description as well. He could have stopped at *life*, but He adds the word *abundantly*. It is life in the strongest terms. It is not mere breathing, existing, having a mundane, boring experience; the life Jesus offers is full, satisfying, richly rewarding, and abundant in every way.

CHAPTER 10—JOURNAL

This chapter looks at deliverance from destruction—evil that goes even beyond terror, arrows, and disease. It is when life is completely destroyed. Psalm 91:5–6 mentions several categories of evil, but destruction takes on the magnitude of an all-out assault. Reflect on how easy or difficult it is for you to believe God will protect you from disaster if you trust Him.

_____

_____

_____

_____

_____

_____

_____

_____

_____

_____

_____

THOUGH A THOUSAND FALL

*A thousand may fall at your side and ten thousand at
your right hand, but it shall not approach you.*

—Psalm 91:7

What Is Happening Around Me?

I had been awakened by a 2:00 a.m. phone call. When my dad was out of town, it was normal for him to call very late to talk to my mom. This time was different. I heard fear in Mom's voice. Suddenly afraid myself, I rose up out of bed to look straight through my bedroom door and into the kitchen where my mom was standing with the phone. I'll never forget the look on her face. I jumped out of bed to ask what happened, and she eventually got off the phone and told me that my dad was involved in a very serious car wreck in which he was hit by a drunk driver.

The next day, we made an eight-hour drive to visit him in a major city hospital, where we found out that my dad was given only a 1 percent chance to live. However, God had other plans, and my dad was soon put into rehab so he could try to make a recovery. So here I was, three years after my dad's wreck, with my family trying to adjust to life with one parent at home and one in a rehabilitation facility. It was hard for all of us, and all we could do was try to cope and keep each other going.

Three years after the accident, I was a sophomore in high school. I had hit sweet sixteen and felt like I was at some sort of peak as far as life being good to me. I had no idea of the challenges that were ahead of me, and I never would have dreamed of the kind of tragedy that was about to strike my life again.

It was homecoming week and everyone was fired up, prepping for the game and getting dates for the dance. I had two friends, Brandy and Kristi, who drove from a town forty miles away to get to school every day, sometimes carpooling and other times making the trip separately. Both were basketball teammates of mine, and we were attending a very small school, so everyone was close.

On Thursday, February 1, Brandy was driving in for school when she rolled her vehicle and was killed. She had been running for basketball homecoming queen as one of the representatives of her junior class. We all knew her well and the news hit us incredibly hard. Everyone loved her. She was always such a sweet and caring girl and she had meant so much to us. Everyone just kept repeating, "Why did this happen to her? She was such a good person." The student body elected her homecoming queen, and her sister accepted the title for her. That was all we could really do.

Later, after the shock had begun to dull, Kristi told me a story. She said, "The week before Brandy was killed, we were driving past the cemetery and Brandy just started yelling and saying, 'Get it off of me. Get it off of me!' Nobody knew what she was talking about, and I just chalked it up to her freaking out about being near the cemetery."

Through this ordeal, I became good friends with Kristi. Best friends, in fact. We were in math class together when we heard that Brandy had been killed on the way to school that day. I felt so sorry for Kristi that my heart went out to her, so we clung to each other and made it through those hard times together. In fact, the whole school banded together and supported one another.

Three months later, on April 30, Kristi saw a couple of friends pass by the window of a classroom and decided to open the window so she could say something to them. It was an old window and hard to open, so she put her right hand on the window above to use it for leverage. Her hand went right through the glass. She turned around and screamed, blood pouring from the gash in her wrist. Acting on instinct, I ran over to her and grabbed her wrist, putting pressure on it to control the bleeding. The doctor later said that decision saved her life; the glass had cut so deeply that it had actually severed an artery. She had major surgery and eventually made a full recovery. Brandy's death was still so fresh that the thought of losing Kristi terrified me.

And then, just one week later, another attack came out of nowhere. Sam, my boyfriend, was killed in a car accident. Sam, who was every sixteen-year-old girl's dream, was older than me—twenty-one in fact. This man was *model material* and when he asked me out on a date, everything in me was saying *yes!* We had been dating a couple of months, and I was out of town. He wrecked his vehicle coming home from a party. He was drunk. The paramedics airlifted him to a major city hospital, but he didn't survive. I felt guilty because I didn't drink and wouldn't let him drink around me, so I couldn't help but think that he wouldn't have been killed if I had been with him.

My heart was already hurting so badly from losing him, and then, just to make a point, the local police station asked permission to have his mangled vehicle towed to the open area across from the school so the kids could see what happens to people who drive drunk. They definitely made their point. I had to look at that gruesome reminder of my loss every day. All of this was almost more than I could bear, and I just kept thinking, "What else can go bad?" This was the time I started drinking, feeling that I had to have something to numb all the pain.

And then, on October 30 of that same year, my grandfather passed away. He had struggled with emphysema for a number of years, but it was still unexpected and, for me, entirely too soon.

I didn't know about God's promises of protection in Psalm 91 at that time in my life. Looking back now, I just feel incredibly *upset* to recognize that the spirit of death gave Brandy a stark forewarning the day she drove by the cemetery. We were all so ignorant of God's Word that no one knew it was a warning. We didn't even know who our enemy was, and we certainly had no idea how to fight him. We are literally living in the times of thousands falling beside us, and I wish I had known about preventative prayer and how to stand on the Lord's promises so I could have fought against that attack on my friend and resisted the enemy through the power of God's promise of protection.

—STEPHANIE LYKINS

FEAR CAN'T SAVE YOU

It's obvious why the police thought Sam's wrecked vehicle would be an effective visual aid to help prevent drunk driving. It was too late for Sam, but maybe the grim reminder would help others. This is how the world thinks of prevention; the scare tactic is a very *raw* form of deterring undesirable behavior.

Do signs that say TEXT, DRIVE, AND DIE and show gory images of car wrecks really prevent accidents? Maybe for a week, but fear doesn't have much staying power. It is simply the drum everyone beats when they have no other drum to beat.

BULLY FEAR

Psalm 91:5–6 builds a strong case against fear—against fear of terror by night, fear of arrows by day, fear of pestilence that stalks in darkness, and fear of destruction that lays waste at noon. And yet fear is often the central factor around which people design their prevention programs.

But consider this truth: not only does fear have little

staying power as a preventative measure, but the Bible says fear can actually draw disaster to us. Proverbs 10:24 warns, "What the wicked fears will come upon him." Job 3:25 makes it even more personal: "What I fear comes upon me, and what I dread befalls me." Isaiah 54:14 challenges us, "You will be far from oppression, for you will not fear; and from terror, for it will not come near you."

Fear will try to *bully* you. Like a bully on a playground, the enemy is drawn to those who fear his terror and destruction. Fear has been called the great magnet, and it's odd, but it can draw the very thing we fear. It can open a door to disaster.

Act on What God Says

Time would prove that fear didn't have the power to prevent more disaster in Stephanie's situation. Even though the world put up its best warning signs, that didn't make Stephanie *not* drink and *not* follow the same path as Sam. Before the wreck, she was a good influence on her friends; after the wreck, she felt herself plummeting into hurt and despair. It was too much. And the others in her crowd who had a semblance of restraint now fell into the same abyss to escape the pain. It was the boldest move the police had, but such a tactic often re-creates the same result.

It has been said (very pessimistically) that you will eventually become what you hate. And likely you've heard stories of people who hated an alcoholic parent yet followed a similar path. The logic doesn't supersede the hurt and pain. The local police hoped the frank reality of showcasing what can happen when you drink and drive would help others face it and make better decisions. A scare tactic like this might be a temporary fix, but often it actually has the opposite effect.

Real prevention arises from what you do with God's Word. The police had a bold idea, but such a tactic often re-creates the same results. Only God's Word can truly reach a hurting heart. When Stephanie pursued a life with the Lord, the downward spiral ended.

Psalm 91:7, which speaks of thousands falling on both sides, is probably the chapter's most recognizable scripture. With its talk of thousands falling to destruction, it seems to be describing a battle scene, but these words are just as applicable to the times in which we live today. You may face a time in your life when everything you know to be solid falls around you. In the face of personal failure, death, divorce, and disasters, nothing seems secure and you can easily find yourself becoming cynical.

God has given you the promises of Psalm 91 to protect you from every kind of evil you may encounter. But it's up to you to believe in God's promises even more strongly than you believe in the things you can perceive physically. (See Ephesians 6:12.) You don't have to be one of the ten thousand who fall *if you will hold fast to God's Word.*

CHAPTER 11—JOURNAL

This chapter reminds us that bad things are happening all around us. Verse 7 is probably the most recognizable promise in Psalm 91. It sounds like a description of a battlefield. Reflect on how you can apply this promise to your life in the days in which we are living.

_____

_____

_____

_____

_____

_____

_____

_____

_____

_____

_____

_____

_____

Chapter 12

UNBELIEVING BELIEVERS

You will only look on with your eyes and see the recompense of the wicked [unbeliever].

—PSALM 91:8

AN EXPERIMENT WITH *VULNERABILITY*

 My life began as a typical good little Christian girl's life would— homeschooled until high school, close family, parents who taught my brother, sister, and me about God and the Bible all the time. Daddy was my hero, Mom was my friend, big brother was the cool kid, and little sister was my very best friend. We were all heavily involved in church activities. From the time I could put a sentence together, I was telling people that I wanted to be a missionary. I knew at quite a young age that missions and ministry were my calling in life.

Church was my absolute favorite part of the week. I was always involved in choir, Bible Drill, the church drama club, AWANAS, youth leadership, mission trips, and the youth worship team, and I even played percussion for our church services on occasion. I was popular and almost always the leader of the pack. I was the one all the kids looked up to and wanted to be friends with, and the kid most parents wanted their children to hang out with—your *typical* perfect, innocent, sweet little church girl.

Ideally a childhood like mine should have produced a godly, straight-laced missionary out of me. But, of course, that is not how the story goes. Two major life changes happened when I was young, which would begin to multiply into a series of problems.

A close relative began experimenting with drugs and different religions at a young age. I remember the first time he locked himself in his room for hours and suddenly ran out screaming that the devil was in his room. The whole family was summoned into his room, and we all began to pray. I remember sensing a disturbing presence. I was afraid, yet curious.

I asked him what he was doing the day he thought the devil was in his room. He told me he got in trouble and was angry at his mom. So he flipped a coin. He decided that if it landed on heads, he would forgive her. But if it landed on tails, he would make a deal with the devil. The coin must have landed on tails. Whatever deal he made with the devil that day would take him down a path of rebellion, anger, drug abuse, witchcraft, and demonic visitations. His behavior really scared me, but I didn't know what to do.

Not knowing much about spiritual warfare, I began watching scary movies, thinking that if I watched enough of them I would eventually go numb and not be afraid anymore. This mind-set began the destructive pattern of numbing my pain and fears instead of facing and dealing with them. This is not the attitude of an overcomer, but of a powerless person.

I became his rescuer. When he would get in trouble, of any kind, I would bail him out. When he was too drunk or high to drive, I would pick him up. When no one could seem to talk or reason with him, I was the one who could. I was his defender and biggest lobbyer. Although there are healthy aspects to being a loyal and protective family member, my relationship with him became a codependent wreck. I would end up enabling him and becoming his crutch. My heroic defensive and protective attitude was actually only giving me a false sense of purpose and value. This codependent-rescuer relationship would only be the beginning of many other unhealthy relationships with men in my future.

The second life-changing issue was my parents' marital struggles. My parents seemingly had a very good marriage, however, one day that security abruptly changed. Dad took responsibility, but the hurt and pain he caused remained. Although they were Christians and committed to marriage, in their flesh was another battle and that did not mean their road to reconciliation was going to be easy or guaranteed. There was tremendous tension between them in the following weeks, that turned into months, that turned into years. I remember crying a lot, but only at first. One night I was lying on my bed crying and suddenly had a thought. "What can crying do to save my parents' marriage? Nothing." I decided that crying was only a weakness and that a tough girl would never cry or allow emotions to rule her. After that night, I refused to allow myself to cry. Eventually I would come to a point where I would no longer be able to conjure up tears. I knew no emotions—not love, not anger, not joy, not pain. This mind-set just fed my desire to live life *numb*.

My parents chose to save their marriage and stay together. I decided that with a marriage to repair and a relative who was out of control, my parents didn't need anything else to worry about. However, this thought would not keep me from being rebellious or making stupid decisions. It would only keep me from being honest with my parents and those around me about what I was really thinking, feeling, and doing.

I decided I was going to handle all of my life's problems on my *own*. I would become Little Miss Independent: proud, tough, and strong. And one day everyone would look at me in amazement that I had the ability to handle so many things in life successfully on my own. My parents would be proud because I had handled things *all by myself*. But this idea only created a two-faced child. To my family and church, I was still the *perfect* Christian girl who never did wrong. And behind the scenes I was the complete opposite. To maintain my two-faced lifestyle, I would have to become a people-pleaser to my parents and friends so they would not see behind the veil.

As a teenager, I began dating guys I never should have hung around. When we broke up, I quickly moved on to another relationship. That would be one of the worst mistakes of my life. I once stayed in an abusive relationship for two years. Then I had abusive boyfriend after abusive boyfriend to feel numb. I'd drink to get numb. And I'd cut myself to be numb. Despite all of this I still believed I could take care of *myself,* my family member, and my parents' marriage all on my *own.* I figured that by lying and not telling anyone about what I was dealing with every day, no one would have to take a break from their problems to help me with mine. And when it would all end, everyone would be impressed with how I handled everything all by myself.

I stayed in the first abusive relationship for a lot of the same reasons I had an unhealthy relationship with my relative—I wanted to be the rescuer of the broken, abusive man. I needed a sense of purpose in life, so I was determined to be the one who could change my boyfriend. Finally the abuse could not be kept a secret anymore—no matter how many lies I told. But when we broke up, I continued my code-pendent rescuer mentality with the next guy…and the next guy, and the next. Instead of my being a res-cuer of men, men became victims of my selfishness.

Only now I had another problem. After the abuse I was love-starved. So now not only did I have a selfish need to find purpose and value in a man, but I also needed to find someone to rescue me. Every relationship that came my way ended in another disappointment—not only could I not rescue anyone, but also no one was ever able to rescue me. Only God can truly rescue.

GOD ENTERS THE STORY

Fortunately in college God brought me to a college group where the students loved me enough to help me work through my messes and mistakes. At twenty-one I decided to begin a journey back to God and my desire to be a missionary. This road would be one of the longest and hardest roads I have ever taken.

This college group paid for me to go to the Philippines for a short mission trip. I flew eighteen hours both ways for an experience that would turn my world upside down. I broke free from the lie that because of my past I had no right to minister to or help people. I came back confident that God could use me right where I was.

But the next lesson would be to separate from my confidence in myself and put my confidence in God. I was on the road to recovery, making strides in some areas while wrestling with other areas. At twenty-two, I was in great need of a job, and I was doing so well with my newfound walk with God, that the next step was a perfect match. I applied for a job at a Christian radio station where my best friend was a DJ. I thought it would be fun to DJ at a radio station, especially the one where my best friend worked. I always excelled in music, theater, speech, debate, and anything else that required standing up in front of a bunch of people. So, of course, I figured being a radio DJ would be no big deal. My college communications professor said I was a natural fit.

Up until this point I had gone through life riding on what was easy. If I was naturally good at something, then of course I would do it. If I was passionate about something, then I would learn to work harder— but never too hard. If I didn't know how to get what I wanted, then I'd use my looks or talk my way into making something happen, or I'd delegate the hard work to someone else. If things got too difficult, I would either find the easy way around it or numb myself to go through it robotically so I wouldn't feel the pain.

I was given a job as the radio host for the evening show. I was thrilled to have the opportunity, but something happened when I got behind the microphone. Suddenly my head started to spin and I couldn't seem to find words for anything. I was a terrible host, from not being able to speak in a proper radio voice to not equipping myself for the spiritual responsibility. I was a mess. All of a sudden I was locked in a world that didn't care what my talents were. My worldly talents and charm were suddenly not good enough anymore.

If I had a weakness or insecurity, it was sure to show itself during my show. I was faced with another level of people-pleasing. I wanted to do radio because it was ministry, but I also still wanted to hold on to the world. I wanted to appear as if I was doing ministry, as I told everyone I wanted to do, while living a worldly life, where I was still numb and trying to fight on my own. All of the lies from my past abuse that I never dealt with began to surface. Every time I got on the air, I'd hear my former boyfriend telling me I was stupid, worthless, and other names. I dealt with an extreme amount of anxiety after my first abusive relationship, and it would rear its ugly head whenever I sat behind that microphone. I was having complete meltdowns and panic attacks during my show that I couldn't explain. And once again I began to feel unworthy of doing any kind of ministry.

Christian radio was not just a job to pay my bills. It was actual ministry. To do real ministry, you need to have intimacy with God. You need to work hard to get filled up so you can pour out. You need to walk the walk you talk and take your place in the kingdom. There's no room and no time for posers in ministry and in the kingdom. No one will last as a faker in ministry. This is a concept I had not yet grasped.

Although I was trying—I was seeking God, I was working toward freedom in my life, and I did want to do ministry—I was not prepared for the journey and the sacrifices I would have to make in ministry. Truth be told, I was not *fully* seeking God. I was still seeking the approval and love of others. I was still putting an unhealthy pull on the guys around me, trying to find a rescuer of my own.

One weekend I chose to help lead a youth camp alongside one of my best guy friends, with whom I had developed yet another codependent relationship. I knew I needed to prerecord my evening show before I could leave for the weekend. But I got caught up in "boy world" and not only forgot to prerecord but also forgot to even tell anyone I was leaving for camp. I remember receiving a phone call at the camp, asking where I was and why there was dead air on the radio. I had no excuse. I knew I'd made a mess once again because I'd chosen men over everything else that was important. Miraculously I was given grace after one of the worst mistakes a DJ can make, and I was able to keep my job. But I didn't last long. Eventually my selfish, insecure, worldly flesh got me fired from Christian radio.

A short time later I got a job working at Chick-fil-A. After working there only three months, I got a raise, which led to another raise and a promotion quickly after that. I excelled at Chick-fil-A, starting at the bottom and quickly working my way to being one of the best employees. I was praised for my hard work, dedication, perfectionism, friendliness, and love toward others. It was such a contrast from my terrible work at the radio station. *Why was it so different at Chick-fil-A?*

The difference for me was that radio was ministry and Chick-fil-A was a business. At the radio station I had to pull on heaven and engage in spiritual warfare. I had to feed listeners with the Word. I was trusted to choose wisely the content of my show and given the freedom to record my show whenever I needed. I could even set my own schedule. At Chick-fil-A, on the other hand, I was given a job description, a set time I had to be at work every day, and daily tasks that did not change. Chick-fil-A did not put a demand on me spiritually. I didn't have to engage in spiritual warfare if I didn't want to. And I wasn't required to grow spiritually in order to get my job done.

Realizing this difference would eventually rock my world. Once again God gave me a reality check on where I was and where I had the potential to go. Should I settle for the world where I excelled, thrived, and was praised? Or should I answer that call on my life for ministry, face my fears and insecurities, and pull on heaven to make a difference in the kingdom? I chose the kingdom. I chose to rise above my fears and take another step toward fulfilling my calling in God's kingdom.

This decision required me to let go of the world and get intimate with God. Layers and layers of sin, darkness, addiction, fear, anxiety, self-medicating, and lies I believed began to peel away, and I started to identify more and more with who God created me to be in His kingdom. I had finally dived deep into the ocean of freedom and healing, and I was ready to do what was necessary to answer God's call on my life.

Eventually I left Chick-fil-A and began working in management. I was excited because this was a new mission field. It felt like a promotion in the kingdom to me. I had moved from working at the Chick-fil-A in the mall to being second in command of the entire mall. My mission field grew from a restaurant to the entire building. God was expanding my influence and trusting me with more. I began ministering to the mall tenants and the shoppers. I would pray over people and evangelize whenever I had the opportunity.

My mind-set had changed from just simply getting the job done and doing what was required of me to making sure I was ministering. I was finally beginning to understand that I would never make it as a "poser" in God's kingdom, and that I would never be able to help bring freedom to others if I wasn't working to receive freedom in my own life. I began making myself push through the laziness of not wanting to fight and not wanting to feel. When I didn't feel like praying over someone

or felt awkward ministering, I would make myself
do it anyway, because it always brought me such a
rewarding feeling in the end.

I remember once working on an important project
in the middle of the mall. An elderly man approached
me with a question. My first thought was that I really
did not have time to talk to this man. But I paused
anyway. He was kind of a grumpy man, and I felt like
God was prompting me to minister to him. Despite
having a project that seemed urgent, I decided to do
what I felt God was asking. So I asked the man if
there was anything I could pray with him about. He
seemed a little shocked at my question at first, but
then he began sharing about his health problems and
telling me he wasn't sure God loved him because of
the life he had lived.

I started ministering to him, sharing with him
why God chooses to love us. The man's wife suddenly came out of nowhere and was grumpy herself. She didn't seem to want to talk about God or
care that her husband was interested in receiving
prayer. Although she kept trying to grab his arm and
leave, he continued to stay engaged in the conversation we were having. So I kept talking. Eventually
the wife stopped and began listening herself. They
both agreed to receive prayer and the man decided to
accept Christ. So I prayed the prayer of salvation with
him, and as we were praying together, I could hear
the wife praying the same prayer with us! The devil
tried to use the wife as a distraction, but God ended
up touching her heart as well! With testimonies like

this increasing in frequency, how could I possibly not want to grow in intimacy with God?

God has been so sweet with His love and grace in my life. Even during my dark times and difficult journey to connect with who He created me to be, God never stopped blessing me with opportunities to pray for and minister to people. God never pulled me out of the game and made me sit on the sidelines until I could behave myself. God always chose to believe in me. My dream of working for a mission organization has been the next step for me, and I am now assigned to work with those caught up in the sex trade in other nations.

Since all of these occurrences I have found love and freedom on levels I didn't know existed. I no longer have a victim mentality or rely on codependent relationships. I no longer live in fear and anxiety. I am full of love. I have embraced the life of being single and content with who I am in Christ, and I no longer feel the desperate need for a man to fulfill me. I no longer feel the need to please and live for others. I know who I am in the kingdom. I have taken my place. I found that God was the rescuer I was looking for.

—LIZA MEYNIG

Liza is one of those rare gems who decided to part ways with a fake life. Instead of going deeper into deception and lying even to herself, Liza decided to get real with the Lord. This vulnerability led to a growing chain of good events that began to occur. And there is a marked turnaround in Liza—and good things began to happen—when her life interracted with love and vulnerablity.

Psalm 91:8, which speaks about the "recompense of the wicked," sounds negative, but really it is a good thing. No one really wants to live in a world of sin without wages (penalties). And most of us can attest that there's no such thing as sin without pain. There is recompense (consequences).

You will see recompense (payment) being doled out at times. There is judgment. There is justice. Every sin will be exposed sooner or later and paid for. An evil dictator falls; a ruthless aggressor is stopped; a tyrant faces his crimes against humanity; a wrong is rectified. The "recompense of the wicked" speaks of justice. The justness of God means that evil will not triumph—that Hitlers do not win, that communistic governments fall, that darkness does not extinguish light.

This verse says we will "only look on and see" it happening. The word "only" indicates detachment, that we will see but not experience the evil, that the evil we see will not get inside of us. We are set apart in that we don't allow our enemy's hate to change us. This verse points to the fact that the evil in the world will not prevail.

It's easy to focus on how bad the world has become. Evil is rampant everywhere we look. There are fakes in the world and even fakes in the church. No one likes a hypocrite—God is clear that He doesn't. And there is such a thing as recompense (people getting what they deserve). In time, wrongdoers will fall, and we might even be smug about their fall; at the very least we will tell ourselves that we saw their demise coming.

We are very quick to judge who the unbeliever is—a liar, a cheater. But perhaps there is such a thing as the *unbelieving* believer—the faker, the poser. One author coined the phrase "the practical [Christian] atheist," meaning if we are not Christians at our core, we just bear the title as an adjective as we live daily without God.[1] When we are living with any amount of hypocrisy, to a degree we are placing ourselves in the category of "the wicked."

This kind of talk sounds negative when we think about *our* hypocrisy becoming exposed. But really it is the most freeing thing that can happen.

Many people think of the gospel as an insurance policy that secures only their eternity, and they live defeated, powerless lives. They are depriving themselves of so much. Many ask only about fire insurance. They want to know, "What do I have to do to avoid hell?" And then they see how close to the edge they can live. Like Liza, many of us have problems or issues, but instead of putting our trust in God, we put it in ourselves and take pride in how strong a situation is making us. Many times it is not making us strong; it is making us hard and numb.

Life with God is more than barely escaping judgment or hell; His Word is a handbook for living an empowered life in this world. God offers us real answers for where we are. If we're on a fast track living a shallow, nonvulnerable life but slapping a Christian label on ourselves, there is still hope. We can experience hope and joy when we let the deepest part of God call out to the deepest part of us—and stop living a life that is fake.

CHAPTER 12—JOURNAL

This chapter talks about living authentically for Christ. Is there an area of your life where you're putting your trust in yourself instead of God?

_____

_____

_____

_____

_____

_____

_____

_____

_____

_____

_____

_____

Chapter 13
NO PLAGUE COMES NEAR MY FAMILY

No harm will overtake you, no disaster will come near your tent.

—Psalm 91:10, niv

Dreams and Prevention

KIM HULL (CENTER) WITH HER FAMILY

It was a shock when Angie came up to me and asked if I was Kim Hull. And what she said next shocked me even more! She had a dream and wanted to share it with me. What struck us both as odd is that in the dream she knew my name and in real life she knew of me, but we had not met. In fact, she had actually gone up to another woman first, asking if she was Kim Hull. She bowed out of that situation by praying over that woman and her family. The woman had a tormenting dream about her family and was glad for the mistaken identity. But now she'd found me, Kim Hull, the person she was looking for.

In her dream, my family was in a terrible car wreck with some fatalities. If Angie didn't already, she now had my complete attention! I was wondering what to do, when she asked if we could stand together in agreement and pray about this dream and what it could mean. We took authority over the spirit of death and harm she had seen in the dream, praying it off of my family and declaring Psalm 91. We also prayed other scriptures that came to mind until we both had a complete release in our spirits and peace in our minds that the danger had been averted and my family was safe in the hands of God. I thanked her, so grateful for what she had done, and, at peace, continued on with my busy life.

The next fall, the Sunday night before school was to start, my car was loaded with my triplet teens and their friends after a back-to-school bash at church. I had just dropped a friend's daughter off after our evening church service. I came to a stoplight near her home and stopped, and when the light turned green I proceeded through the intersection on my way to drop off another teen. Out of nowhere, a drunk driver going sixty-five miles an hour down the main street in our small town hit the front passenger side of my car. Everything happened quickly, but we hung on as we were completely spun around on two tires in the middle of the intersection before our vehicle came to rest and started smoking. I quickly urged the four kids to get out of the car and head to the grass on the side of the road. My car was demolished, but we walked away from a wreck that could have been devastating. One of the young men, a friend's son, bumped his elbow and later discovered that he had a small fracture that had to be cast, but that was the only injury.

I believe with all my heart that if Angie had not shared her dream and prayed for the members of my family, that wreck's outcome would have been totally different. Our vehicle had been T-boned and pushed up on two wheels. We had been hit so hard that our car was pushed onto another street, and the passenger side where my son and his friend were sitting was completely caved in—yet we walked out alive! When we went to see the car the next day at the wrecking yard, we were shocked that everyone survived because the right side was demolished—we were truly witnessing a miracle as we surveyed the damage.

After seeing the car, I remembered the prayer that Angie had prayed and knew I needed to tell her what had happened. I quickly drove to her office and banged on the glass window to get her attention. In the middle of a meeting, she came out to see what the commotion was about and I offered to take her to see the car and hear the report. The men at the wrecking yard had asked how many died in the wreck. We both knew that God had answered our prayer when we took authority over Angie's warning dream and that His promises of protection *over my tent* had come full circle from the time we had prayed.

What happens when we have a tormenting dream? I had never thought in terms of *doing something about it* as a preventative measure. If I had a bad dream or a sudden or passing thought about someone, it had never seemed more than coincidental, but now I know it can be a warning, reminding us to pray. Having the promises of Psalm 91 is such a blessing, and we can pray them at the first hint that something might be coming against us.

—KIM HULL

GOD WANTS TO PROTECT THOSE AROUND YOU

What a wonderful dimension to this promise in Psalm 91, that "no disaster will come near your tent" (v. 10, NIV). We can believe God and receive protection for our families. In Kim's case, her tent was her car! Think of how Rahab must have felt in Joshua 2, when God allowed her to bring her extended family into her house, where they were protected from harm. In a similar way, God has made us promises that provide for the safety of our families if we will trust Him.

Proverbs 3:29 tells us, "Do not devise harm against your neighbor, while he lives securely beside you." So include others in this "tent," including your neighbors. Let the differences go and pray for your siblings, other family members, and friends. Take note of the people you do life with—from sports to work to organizations and clubs to Bible study groups and worship teams! Think about the fact that they may not have anyone else in their lives praying for them. Your extended family needs your prayers. Pray for those who are over you since you are under their authority. They need prayer. They are also a part of your "tent" or dwelling.

FROM *WORRY* TO *PEACE*

Sometimes it's hard not to worry about your family. Stop the worrying and start praying. Have you ever been troubled by the thought of someone close to you dying? That is a horrible feeling. Pray until you get a peace about the person's safety. Psalm 91:10 moves the concept of protection from the individual and "stretches out the tent pegs," so to speak. God tells you that "no disaster will come near your tent." It is a good promise to claim.

A Brother's Love

One story that warms my heart every time I think of it is the story of the Velez brothers who were all sent to different foster homes at a young age. The father had been sent to prison for abusing the boys, and their mother had died when the boys were little. No one wanted to take all the boys, so they were separated and sent in four different directions.

Throughout his growing-up years, Gilbert, next to the oldest, had fantasized of one day being reunited with his brothers. That, of course, was an impossibility—where were they? Who did they live with? Surely by now even their names had changed.

The Velez story intersected with ours during a Brownwood parade. Two guys ran into Gilbert Velez, who was now twenty and living alone. They led him in the prayer of salvation and invited him to come to one of their college Bible studies. At the next meeting Gilbert was one of the first to arrive, blending into the group as though he had always been there.

Gilbert told everyone about his separated brothers and how he believed they would all be together again one day. Gilbert began devouring the Bible, and he found the story of Hannah in 1 Samuel chapter 1. When he read that Hannah promised God that if He would give her a child, she would give him back to the Lord, Gilbert took that as a word from God. He told the Lord that if He would return his brothers to him, he would give them back to God.

A friend of his deceased mother wrote to a case-worker she knew in Dallas. Through a series of letters Gilbert found that one of his brothers, Jesse, had been in prison, and after his release had been homeless on the streets of Dallas for three months. Even though Gilbert had been estranged from Jesse for six years, God supernaturally made a way for Gilbert to find Jesse (and move him into the apartment with him), get him involved in the college group, and lead him in giving his life to Jesus. Another series of difficult events opened the door for the next brother, Joseph, to be found in Dallas and reunited with Gilbert and Jesse. God was on a roll. It was only a couple of months after that when they found their last brother, Samuel, in Fort Worth. When arrangements were made and it was time to pick Samuel up, Gilbert's car had broken down. Nonetheless, as only God can do, a neighbor loaned the brothers his Cadillac Escalade so they could make the trip in style.

Gilbert has played the role of mother and father, and true to the promise he made to God, he introduced each one of his brothers to the Lord. They all have jobs, and some have taken college courses. They go on mission trips with the college group, and they pray their hearts out whenever someone has a need. The night that I saw all four brothers together for the first time, they were all dressed up in three-piece suits—looking like the King's kids that they are.

On one of the college outings, all four of the boys were in the same van headed to Miami to evangelize the Cubans in that area. It was on that trip that Jesse got separated from the group. Their phones were dead, and the brothers were ready to panic—how could they find each other among those thousands of people? But they began to pray and claim God's promise about lost sheep. God answered their prayers and once again joined them in a tearful reunion. When it was his turn to preach at one of their college meetings, Jesse used the prodigal son story in Luke 15 as his text and told how God was faithful to find him, a prodigal son, in a lost and dying world and bring him home.

Gilbert has kept his promise. God gave him his brothers, and he has given them back to God. How heartwarming it is to see them all together—loving and serving God.

—Peggy Joyce Ruth and Gilbert Velez

The beauty of Psalm 91 is that when we pray for more than ourselves, we bring our whole families under the shield of God's Word. We exercise a certain amount of authority for those under our roof as we apply the richness of this covenant to our entire household.

CHAPTER 13—JOURNAL

This chapter explores God's provision for our family's safety. His protection extends not just to us as individuals but also to those who dwell with us. Who are some of the people you pray for regularly? Take some time to pray and ask God if anyone else should be added to your list.

_____

_____

_____

_____

_____

_____

_____

_____

_____

_____

_____

_____

Chapter 14

ANGELS KEEP GUARD

He shall give His angels charge over you to guard you in all your ways. They shall bear you up in their hands, lest you strike your foot against a stone,

—PSALM 91:11–12, MEV

IT'S COMFORTING TO know that God involves Himself in the minute details of our lives even when we may be caught off guard or "lost in the moment." The latter would describe Justin McFarland and the team of college students he was leading as they plunged into the pristine waters of a waterfall deep in the jungle.

WHERE HAS THE ENEMY GONE?

After having ministered to the little village at the foot of the mountain in Chiapas for a couple of days, the team decided to make the hike through the bush up to the fabulous waterfalls that the villagers had recom-

JUSTIN AND HEATHER MCFARLAND

mended before returning to home base. They were told the falls were about one hour away and the children would lead them. Three hours later the team was relieved to find they were nearing the destination.

Hearing the falls long before they reached them,

the students felt their enthusiasm mount as they approached. When they broke through the foliage to the banks of the river, the group exploded with "Oohs" and "Wows." In an instant, shoes and socks were shucked and bodies were smashing into the once-quiet pool of cool jungle water. The students climbed the falls one tier at a time until they could see the top level. At the base of the top tier was a massive pool of deep, cold water nearly five hundred feet wide.

The hot, muggy jungle air drove the students into the deep pool, and they paddled toward the prize of the beautiful top cascade. After gloating in their accomplishment, they dived from the rocks and enjoyed the cool refreshment of the pools for several hours. With the curiosity of young guys, they investigated the entire area, making quite a commotion in their youthful antics. Some of the students were puzzled that no locals had accompanied them in their swim across the deep pool to the top of the falls. Justin and the rest of the students, however, had been so energized by the thought of reaching the very top that they hadn't even noticed their companions hadn't participated in the swim. The native children would sporadically clap their hands above their heads as if they were chomping down and seemed to be afraid of the water. The team thought, "Poor kids, we'll teach them to swim next year!"

It wasn't until the next return trip, when Justin visited the village, that he asked why the children had not joined in the swim. He was told that huge migratory crocodiles guarded the bigger pools of water. The locals had been quite impressed that the team was brave enough to chance the big pool and its deep water. The students, of course, were horrified and wanted to know why they hadn't been warned of the crocodiles. After all, the locals had told the team about the pool and the children guided them to it. Since the team had charged ahead into the water without asking, either the locals assumed the swimmers knew what they were doing, and the children, were extremely delighted with the possible danger, or the children were trying to warn them. Some things are lost in translation, however, and Justin and his team will never know for sure this side of heaven. After the initial shock of discovering they could have been eaten by crocodiles, the team realized just how faithful God is and how reliable His covenant promise is to those who believe. The villagers were petrified about the culebra or "jungle viper," a vicious snake that shared these pools as well. Who knows what dangers lurked below the waters of those remote jungle falls? The locals certainly knew enough not to swim there.

—BASED ON AN INTERVIEW
WITH JUSTIN MCFARLAND

We rejoice to know that God's protection follows us not only into the known but also into the unknown. Like the ignorant enthusiasm of our student group in the jungle, sometimes we get caught up in the moment and don't even pause to pray for protection. Even though the trip was blanketed with prayer, we knew God's angels had done something special when we found out all the locals were petrified of the submerged crocodiles. Thankfully, God is faithful and merciful to honor His covenant protection of Psalm 91 even when we overstep our bounds just a bit.

How important it is to know beyond a shadow of a doubt that God's promises of protection are absolutely true and reliable—and can deliver us no matter what we may be facing.

GOD MADE ANGELS TO PROTECT YOU

Up until now we have just looked at promises, now we are looking at something God has provided for our protection that is an agent with a special assignment. God has provided special bodyguards to protect us from danger. For those that are not sure that protection for us is near to the heart of God we need to think about His creation of angels. The concept of protection is not just an afterthought, but God has assigned our protection as a responsibility to someone. He actually created an unseen security detail to enforce His desire to protect us and *keep one foot from dashing against a stone*. What a commitment to our protection God has made in assigning angels to each one of us.

What an unbelievable thought that not only did God give us His promises for protection but He made these unique beings to carry it out. If you have any question inside of you that God desires you to live and to serve Him, this creation attests to His willingness to help us through heaven's unseen bodyguards. Whether we know about them or not, they perform the Word of the Lord. So we see that

He gives us a double reinforcement of His protection—His Word and His angels assigned to watch over us.

> Bless the LORD, you His angels, mighty in strength, who perform His word, obeying the voice of His word!
> —PSALM 103:20

Of all the things that Psalm 91 could tell us about the description of the angel's job, it tells us the most minute exacting detail—in regards to our feet. Angels lead us away from stumbling blocks. Psalm 91:12 uses strong verbs—"guard you," "bear you up"—to describe something that seems relatively simple...keeping our feet from stumbling. But their role is more powerful than that; angels give us a way of escape, sometimes lifting us completely out of the way of a fall.

The Bible talks about God's angels all through the Old and New Testaments. They are mighty beings—so strong that one angel can overcome more than a thousand men. They are ready at all times to carry out God's will and to watch over God's people.

> Are they not all ministering spirits sent out to minister to those who will inherit salvation?
> —HEBREWS 1:14, MEV

Sometimes, instantly, we know exactly what God has delivered us from. Other times, we discover what we've been rescued from later, much like the team of college students when they found out they'd been swimming in a crocodile-infested pool in the jungle. And still other miraculous rescues we won't learn about until we get to heaven.

CHAPTER 14—JOURNAL

This chapter took a close look at heaven's bodyguards provided for us. What does it mean to you to know that God has assigned angels to watch over you?

_____

_____

_____

_____

_____

_____

_____

_____

_____

_____

_____

_____

AUTHORITY OVER THE ENEMY

You will tread upon the lion and cobra, the young lion and the serpent [dragon] you will trample down.

—Psalm 91:13

It's Never Too Late to Resist the Enemy

As a preacher's kid and a young Christian, I wasn't doing so badly. I started a Bible study in my school in my junior high years, and even started Bible studies on my high school campus during my freshman year.

One day as I was putting up See You at the Pole posters on campus, I heard a football player inviting people to a big party he had planned.

"Hey, how's it going?" I asked him when we saw each other, just trying to be friendly, hoping he would come.

He responded by saying, "I'd invite you to this party we're having, but you're a preacher's kid. You wouldn't come anyway. You're too good for that!"

When he said "preacher's kid," something inside of me just screamed out silently, "I'll show you preacher's kid!" I was hurt that he wouldn't invite me. I guess I wanted acceptance. Something in me just said, "I'll show you!" and wow did I show them!

From that small comment he made, I took it as a personal challenge and started following the wrong crowd. By the end of my freshman year I was totally mixed up with them. I remained far away from the Lord as I stayed a part of fast living through my whole sophomore year.

One night during that year I was out riding around with a friend in his car. He had done a bunch of drugs and had been drinking earlier that night and was acting crazy. Something I said to him really infuriated him. He decided he was going to kill us both. In a rage he gunned the gas. At this top speed the small car left the road, roared through a field, and headed straight for a tree.

I tried to talk to him, get him to slow down, but he just wouldn't listen to me and turned the music on the radio up full blast. I was petrified. I was afraid I really was going to die, and I knew I was not living for the Lord at that time.

I desperately called out to God, saying, "I know I'm not living for You right now, Lord, *but You are going to have to make this stop.*" Desperately I prayed, "Stop in Jesus' name."

The music was so loud there was no way my friend could have heard what I was saying. I was facing the window on my side and crying out to God. But the instant I finished that prayer, he took his foot off the gas, put it on the brake, and turned away from that tree. God had miraculously delivered me from the enemy's trap. When I asked him what made him stop, he mumbled a confused, "I don't know." He was shocked himself.

During my time away from God, I had a few more close calls that almost took my life, but still I hadn't made a clean break with the world. I had been taught about the authority God gives a believer and would pray at the last moment, taking a big chance that I was playing it too close.

By the end of my sophomore year, I was so miserable that I was done with the wrong crowd—all I wanted was to once again start living for the Lord. It took me nearly all of my junior year to cut off all the wrong relationships and once again be consistent in my living for the Lord. But by the time I started my senior year, I had finally remolded my Christian testimony and was no longer susceptible to the enemy's traps. It's hard to believe I let one stupid comment throw me off. College has been a very good experience for me because I have gotten through my rebellious living without getting killed and have started living the wild adventures that God has planned for my life!

—KAYLA BARNETT BILL

Sometimes believers, especially teens, struggle to do the right thing, and instead yield to the enemy's attacks. Almost every teen struggles with being accepted by his peers. This is what happened to Kayla, a freshman high school student, who was also a pastor's kid and had been actively living for Jesus. Kayla had been taught her authority and knew it, but she laid it down and quit *treading* on evil and fell to it. Even though Kayla gave into the *acceptance and belonging to the in-crowd trap*, God was faithful to her and when she

needed His deliverance the most, He saved her from possible death the instant she called upon Him.

Always remember that your deliverance from the temptation and traps that Satan wants to pull you into is just
one call away. It took Kayla almost losing her life for her to
pick up her authority again. Loudly and boldly affirm, "The
Lord is my refuge and fortress. I trust in You, Lord. I know
You will save me from any traps Satan has set to ensnare
me when I call upon your name."

YOU WILL *TREAD UPON* AND *TRAMPLE DOWN*

Verse 13 of Psalm 91 promises that because of God's protection you will not merely tiptoe through the traps Satan sends
your way—you will tread upon them and trample them down
to ruin. This doesn't just mean you'll rise above the everyday
problems that may trip us up normally; it means you will be
able to run right over the top of life-threatening situations.

> Behold, I [Jesus] have given you authority to *tread*
> upon serpents and scorpions, and over all the power
> of the enemy, and nothing will injure you.
> —LUKE 10:19, EMPHASIS ADDED

As believers, we have God-given authority over the dangers in our lives, whether these dangers are lions, snakes,
or peer pressure. Many people, especially younger people,
have never seen a believer use any spiritual authority, so
they believe the Christian life is void of any real power.
Seeing powerless Christians has led them to believe there
is not much they can do about their problems. What a

life-changing difference it makes when we realize that God has indeed given us authority over harmful elements in our lives.

SHE MUST *HATE* YOU

So many times we have a great goal, but we aren't prepared for what we will face in attaining it because we don't understand our authority as believers.

During her last year in college, Jennifer McCullough asked me to be her mentor and was enjoying our one-on-one times tremendously, especially the scriptures we studied together. I hadn't even met Jenn until five weeks before graduation, so we had a very late start when she announced she felt called to go to Africa for the summer. As she was frantically preparing, Jenn mentioned to a friend of ours, who I'll call Dana, how excited she was to be going to Africa. Dana asked her if she had heard of Psalm 91. When Jenn said no, you would think Dana would have offered to share it with her. Instead, Dana surprised Jenn in the way only Dana can: "Angie must *hate* you not to have told you about Psalm 91!"

Jenn made a beeline for me and asked me why I hated her. I laughed. I was meeting with Jenn two times a week and already felt overwhelmed with how much she had to learn in her discipleship before she graduated—I hadn't even thought about Psalm 91. I solved the problem by giving Jenn my mom's audio teaching on Psalm 91, and Jenn wore out the tape listening to it. Who knew that when she went to Africa her very life would depend on her using those verses to claim authority over the devil's schemes. That, however, is another story...[1]

—ANGELIA RUTH SCHUM

Dana had made a tongue-in-cheek remark about Jenn's ignorance of Psalm 91 in order to get her attention. But the truth is, many congregations have never heard even one sermon on Psalm 91 or on the authority of the believer. Christians are not prepared for the battle they will face in life. Many have never heard of spiritual warfare. Someone has quipped that if a person has not heard about spiritual warfare, then she or he is already a prisoner of war.

Many Christians feel powerless in their lives, largely due to poor discipleship. Can you hear Dana? "Your church must *hate* you if you have never heard a sermon on Psalm 91!" Take the time to seek out and study the authority you have been given. Thank the Lord Dana said something—for who knew that by the end of the summer, Jenn's life would depend on her knowing the protection promised us in Psalm 91. It is verse 13 of Psalm 91 that most spells out our authority.

LIONS, SNAKES, AND DRAGONS

Obviously, God doesn't intend for us to make a habit of provoking lions or poisonous snakes, but He uses these deadly creatures in Luke 10:19 to show us exactly how much authority He means for us to have. To have authority over your circumstances means you have the *right* to do something about them. You have the right to use the name of Jesus to fight off evil the enemy sends against you.

Satan is described as being like a roaring lion, and that image is used here to give you an idea of one of the forms his attacks might take. The attack of an *adult lion* is sudden, loud, powerful, and ferocious. This represents when the devil assaults you head-on and tries to overwhelm you with sheer force. It includes those all-out assaults in your life that make you shudder. In those times the attack is designed to take you out with one blow.

The attack of the *young lion* in Psalm 91:13 is distinctly different from the adult lion's attack. The young lion represents the constant bombardment of small punches that can wear you down. This kind of attack pummels you with a multitude of problems and you can't seem to get back on your feet; often you just want to quit. Jesus didn't let Satan's three attacks in the wilderness (Luke 4:1–13) pile up; instead, He took them one at a time. The attacks only pile up when you don't face each one with the Word or don't actively resist them, or when you fall into temptation and several more come along with it. Avoidance is the worst way to respond to a young lion attack. Separate your attacks by resisting them as they come and don't let them pile up.

The cobra represents a far subtler attack, striking when you least expect it and from a direction you never would have anticipated. Its like when someone tells lies about you behind your back, and it hits you unexpectedly. The puncture wounds from cobra fangs can be hard to detect at first.

Although no one sees the poison as it travels through a body, the results are often deadly. This verse promises the ability to tread without being bitten, so when you walk through dangerous places, stay prayed up and use your authority.

The serpent of old, *the dragon*, is a formidable enemy with the power to trample and destroy those it attacks. The attack of the dragon represents something that is feared but that doesn't face us every day—vain imaginations, a ghost from the past. At the other end of the spectrum, we know some people who are so afraid of bugs that they won't go on the mission field. Behind this concept of trampling down dragons and serpents is the promise that you will not be harmed—indeed, *you will be the one trampling down* these fearsome creatures. Of all the verses in Psalm 91, verse 13 speaks of our ability to tread upon and trample down our problems. It speaks of our authority over attacks intended to harm us.

To make this concept practical, think in terms of playing offense or defense. Any coach knows that both are important. Yet many people are barely making it each day because they are playing just defense. Psalm 91:13, however, shows us another way to live, a way to play offense against the enemy's assaults.

As a follower of Christ, you can use your God-given spiritual power to tread on *all* the powers of the enemy.

CHAPTER 15—JOURNAL

This chapter examines the authority we have as believers. It talks about treading on four different types of creatures. God is not telling us to walk on animals, but rather He is giving us instructions for how to overcome problems and fears that attack us. Spend some time reflecting on the authority God has given you as a believer. How does understanding this authority affect your view of the obstacles you face in life?

_____

_____

_____

_____

_____

_____

_____

_____

_____

BECAUSE I LOVE HIM

"Because he has loved Me, therefore I will deliver him.
—Psalm 91:14, EMPHASIS ADDED

THE MAN BETWEEN ME AND GOD

Why do we sometimes give someone or something else more of our love than we give to God, when deep inside we already know it is not going to end well? Honestly, I never thought it could happen to me. I guess I would have to say, looking back, that I went to sleep on duty when I should have been on guard.

I became a believer at a young age, and I never saw a time coming when I would compromise my convictions. I was too strong for that. Yet, when I look back on it now, I can see that it happened pretty quickly and I didn't put up a very big fight. I was sixteen when I first met him. We were both at a camp and started out as "just friends," as people say. He was handsome, with olive skin and light brown eyes, and attraction wasn't something I'd been taught how to fight. He was very much wanted by other girls and I was proud to be seen with him. But to him, I was a challenge, a strong woman with a strong fence around my heart. Before too long, we were spending every moment together. He had a very good voice and could sing until I melted. He wasn't a believer, but he let me talk to him about the Lord, and even that seemed to pull us closer.

Little by little, I became completely dependent on

him, to the point that nothing and no one else mattered. My need for him was an obsession, and it ran so deep that I felt I couldn't even breathe without him there. Within a couple of years, I had sunk into an artificial world with this man at the center; God was long since forgotten.

Needless to say, my parents didn't approve, but that meant very little to me by then. My relationship with them had become shallow and superficial. I accepted what I needed from them to survive and took nothing else. On some level, I knew my way of life was wrong. I knew it was empty. I just didn't care.

By the time I turned eighteen, I lived in my own secret world. I had reached a point where I simply put God's voice on mute. I no longer spent any personal time with God. We had been an incredibly close family, but now all they got from me was my anger. When I came in, I asked for money and the keys to the car, and then good-bye! My connection with my family was a wreck. But my parents kept praying over me and claiming scriptural promises over my life.

Sometimes, on the occasions when my boyfriend and I would fight, I would go to a friend's house. It didn't matter if it was the middle of the night—I would burst in with my problems. Even though my friend was not a believer, she was the first one to notice a change in me, even though I didn't see it when she first pointed it out. It wasn't until my boyfriend and I had a conversation about his future, and how I fit into it, that fear formed a crack in my obsession. I was suddenly afraid of losing God. Losing the truth. And losing myself forever…and then I found myself praying. All I could ask was, "God, if You're here, please help me find the way back to You." I knew God didn't owe me anything, and I didn't think it would do much good or change my course, but I felt that I had to try.

After I finally turned back to God, I began to see the truth. I had developed a soul tie with this man, and it ran so deep that it took a long time before I was able to break it. Every time I tried, he would be so sweet and so kind that I would let him back in. It wasn't until later that I realized God was trying to teach me not to choose pleasing people over pleasing Him. Eventually, I learned that lesson with this relationship.

I've been on my renewed walk with God for almost three years now, and I've been amazed to see how He can turn all things I had messed up back to His will—even after I had sinned and walked away from Him. Since I learned to put God first, I have formed healthy relationships and renewed old ones, and my life is the best it has ever been.

—MIRIAM

It is possible to *think* we love God but not really know Him well at all. Miriam slowly replaced her love for God with the love of a man. The scary thing is that she didn't even notice she had lost her love for the Lord. It took a friend noticing a negative change and one of those "uncomfortable relationship talks" for Miriam to see that something wasn't right. Her boyfriend was an obsession she became dependent on, and she lost herself—then God broke in through one small crack by way of a conversation. Isn't it great to know the Lord still chases after us even when we have replaced Him with someone or something else?

Sometimes we overspiritualize loving God. Deep love has action and passion attached to it. It is not theoretical, but rather something that takes place in our hearts. The action and the passion involve every part of us—our heart, soul, mind, and strength. Ask yourself, "Do I deeply love God? Do I take time to show the Lord that I love Him?" We realize that our relationships with other people require continual communication and mutual sharing of love, but sometimes we forget that our relationship with the Lord needs to be this intentional.

In Psalm 91:14–16, God Himself is talking to you directly, and He offers seven promises to anyone who truly loves Him. Ask yourself, "Do I really love the Lord?" Be honest with your answer; God already knows it.

LOVE SHOWS

How much we love God shows in how we live our lives. Do you remember when Jesus asked Simon Peter in John 21:15, "Simon…do you love Me?" Think of how embarrassed Simon Peter must have felt when Jesus asked him this question over and over. God is asking you that same question, because He has some amazing promises for the one who truly loves Him.

Jesus went on to tell Peter how to show his love. When Peter said he loved the Lord, it wasn't enough. Jesus said Peter's love would show in how well he took care of those put in his charge. Our love for God shows in how well we love each other.

Humans were literally created to provide company for

the Lord. Just think about it. David was only a teenager when he spent his nights out in the field watching over his sheep, playing his harp, and singing love songs to the Lord. David's love for God was one of the reasons God called him "a man after My heart" (Acts 13:22).

What God wants most from you is for you to spend time talking to Him, listening to Him, and having fellowship with Him. The more time you spend with God, the more you will learn to trust Him and know that His Word is true. David learned to trust God, and that is why he was not afraid to fight the lion and the bear, and later, the giant Goliath. God had become his best friend, and he knew *God would never leave nor forsake him.*

Give yourself to Him completely—give Him your love, your identity, and your life—and let Him be your guide.

> For nothing will be impossible with God.
>
> —LUKE 1:37

For the young person who truly loves the Lord, the reward of that love is the promise that God will protect, deliver, and rescue His beloved. Our love for God puts us in a unique position with Him. With David, it moved him from the fields to the palace to the throne.

During the young adult years, people are making up their minds about how much of their lives they are willing to give to God. Each young person reaches a point when he or she must decide, "Am I going to sell out to God? And if I do, will God return His love to me?" Have you reached this pivotal point in your life?

CHAPTER 16—JOURNAL

This chapter describes how our love for God puts us in a unique position with Him, a position in which we are able to receive His promises. How do you show your love for God?

_____

_____

_____

_____

_____

_____

_____

_____

_____

_____

_____

_____

_____

_____

GOD IS MY DELIVERER

Because he has loved Me, therefore I will deliver him.
—PSALM 91:14

BREAKING THE POWER OF CUTTING

I was sixteen the first time I ever cut. It was my birthday. All my life I'd felt a lot of hurt toward my mother for not being around. The anger and pain just built up and I didn't know how to release it. Sometimes I would just yell into my pillow to get the hurt out. And I would sing a lot. It could be any song that I felt related to my situation. I would just sing it over and over again, and I would feel every bit of it. The singing helped, but the relief was never permanent. I could never find a way to escape all the pain I felt.

I'd known of girls who were cutting since junior high school, and I used to think, "That's weird. Why are they doing that?" But in high school I began to think that might be something I wanted to try. On my sixteenth birthday, I was alone in my room, hurt that my mother had forgotten to call me again or even send a card or a present. And it was the sixteenth time she had forgotten. Then I remembered how the girls in junior high used to say cutting replaces the emotional pain with physical pain and I thought, "That's control."

So I cut for the first time. I didn't feel a release, but I felt control that I hadn't felt before, a control of the pain, and I decided this is how I would release the pain if it got too bad. Anybody else can leave you, but it is different when a parent leaves you. It does something to you. It hinders your ability to love. It makes you feel like you weren't good enough to love. And everything proves it—your grades, your family. My mother didn't even seem to remember my birthday.

This went on for five years. I was constantly cutting and hiding it with a shirt or makeup. But it was always a temporary fix. The cutting made me feel numb, because it shifted my focus from the emotional pain to the physical. And if I got an infection, that was all the better, because it would cause more physical pain and make my emotions feel more numb. I couldn't cry, couldn't feel anything. Depression pills had the same effect. But the emotional pain never actually went away. It kept building. The enemy takes one open door and makes things worse from there. The first door that opened in my life was abandonment and hurt, and it went on to cutting and to more hurt.

Then one day while I was working at a snow cone stand my friend's dad owned, I saw all these people doing a fundraiser. I noticed a guy who was cute, and I thought, "I'm going to go home with him tonight." I had been attracted to men at a very early age. But when I went over to him, it was like he wasn't quite processing that I was flirting with him. So he started talking to me about the mission trip they were going to in the Philippines, and I thought, "OK, I'll play the part." So I asked him what church he was with, and he invited me to a campus ministry. And because I'd never been rejected by a guy before, I thought, "How dare he? I have to get to know him now." It was a challenge.

So I went to the campus ministry, and I remember feeling such pain during the worship, like a stinging pain. It hurt my whole body to listen to the worship leaders sing about this love the Lord had. I had never heard the songs—everything was all new. And I was so uncomfortable. But I remembered how I used to sing to release pain, and I thought, "Maybe I should do that again."

I didn't see the guy I'd tried to flirt with anywhere, and I thought, "That rotten liar." Then I looked and saw him in the sound booth, and I thought, "OK. I'm going to stay here till the end." I found a spot by the fish tank because I didn't want to be seen, and the guy came out of the sound booth and started talking to me. He wanted to know how I liked the service and if I was going to be back at the snow cone machine later, and I told him I wouldn't because it was closed. What I really wanted him to think was that he'd never see me again, to try to entice him again, but he wasn't having any of it. I had my "fake it till I make it" plan going. I felt so heartless and like such a monster. I had always planned to leave the ministry before anyone found out what I was really like, but this time it wasn't working.

I kept going to the campus ministry, because even though the worship songs felt like sandpaper on me, I liked being there. It sounds crazy, but the burn I felt was a good burn. It wasn't like the burn of cutting; it was totally different. I didn't hurt. I can't really explain. It was like I was constantly drawn to it. So even when the college ministry house wasn't open, I would stand outside until someone would come to open it.

Up to that point I had heard three sermons from Angie. One of the sermons was about getting real with the Lord and wrestling things out with Him. I thought, "I've got some things to wrestle out. I'm going to next level with *this* Lord. I'm tired of talking to guys. All these guys, I don't want them!" So I said, "Lord, *You* show me who to talk to! Just highlight, if You will, somebody for me to talk to." And suddenly, all the lights turned off, even in the fish tanks, and the only thing I could really see was Hannah by herself with an empty chair beside her.

I thought, "He did it. He's real! Oh my gosh!" I decided to hold up my end, so I went over to Hannah, and said, "Hey, you don't know me and I don't know you, but the Lord just told me that you would know how to talk to me."

It turns out she had a bunch of sisters, and I thought that's why the Lord directed me to her. So I told her a little bit about what I had been going through, not that I was cutting but about the abandonment and hurt from my mom. And she told me that I needed to go on a date with the Lord. And I was like, "You're crazy. There's no such thing. How do you even do that?" But she said, "Trust me." And she handed me money to pay for my date with the Lord. I thought, "I've been paid to go on a date…with the Lord. So weird."

I decided to go back-roading; that sounded like a date to me. So I used the money she gave me to fill up my truck, and I got a little Lunchable and went on this date with the Lord. I drove until it was just me and the stars and my tailgate. I parked out somewhere by Ten Mile, and I hopped in the bed of the truck. For the first time ever, I was completely alone, and I felt something drop, and I felt the burning without the worship music. I thought, "What is going on?" So I texted Hannah a few times and asked her what was happening. I told her, "I did what you said. This is the dumbest thing ever. It feels so weird." She called me back because I needed coaching since I had never properly dated before. I told her, "Something's wrong, because I don't feel like I'm alone." And she told me, "It's OK. The Lord's there, and you're safe. So whatever you're feeling, just feel it. Just be in the moment. Like you are on a date. You remember what it feels like to go on a date?" I thought, "Kinda. I've never really been on an official date."

So I did what she said, and it's like the Lord started to play out my life. He showed me where all the hurts were coming from and why the burning of worship felt better than the burning of cutting and why it was good for me. And He started telling me that I wasn't abandoned, that He had always been there. He is still telling me things about that night. He said I never had to cut; that was never part of His plan for my life. All the pain, it was never supposed to be there. By taking my mom out of the picture, it was breaking a generational curse of addiction. He was protecting me. He knew how long it would take for her to come around. And by the time she came around there would have been so much hurt, it would have taken me just as long to heal.

I went home after this date to my empty bedroom and just cried. Then the Lord started showing me on that cold December night that He never intended for me to have so much pain. He showed me that at every painful moment in my life, He was there. He was there at every important life event my mother missed. Every time I screamed into a pillow, His arms were ready for me, waiting for me to just let His love in. That night in my bed I let the walls down. I gave Him the pieces of my heart that I had left, and He promised to gladly accept all the other pieces as they came together. I was accepted. I gave my heart and life to the Lord that night in December 2012.

The next year I married a wonderful man and we were expecting a baby. I had been completely delivered of cutting after some leaders from the campus ministry prayed over me for several hours, but two days before my daughter was born I was overcome by those thoughts and cut again. I was in so much pain that day. Sometimes it comes back and knocks. I believe I was under attack. Here I was about to have a daughter, and I just kept thinking about how my mother left us. Before I was even a year old, she'd leave me on the kitchen counter for my four-year-old brother to take care of me.

The pain was so intense it seemed like I was going through postpartum depression before I even had Addy. After all the years, all the pain I'd felt came back in a moment. I thought, "I can't handle this. I could never leave my daughter. I can't understand how my mother did that." Satan really started wearing on me, telling me I was going to be exactly the same as my mom and that it would take years for my daughter to get over the pain I'd already caused her. He kept telling me she was going to ask about the scars on my wrists, and I'd have to explain them to her, and then she'd think, "Well, Mommy did it, so I can cut too." I thought, "I have to stop it before it ever starts." So that was the last time that I ever cut.

A few weeks after I had my daughter, I went to church, and a woman noticed the cuts on my wrists. I put makeup on them, but I guess I didn't do as good a job as I thought. I was so unhappy, and I was physically and emotionally drained because I was still thinking I wasn't equipped to be a good mom. But this woman walked up to me and grabbed my hand and said, "You are worth more than this. You are worth more! You're worth more for that baby girl. You're worth more for your husband. But take them out of the picture. I want you to go home today and look at yourself in the mirror." She couldn't possibly have known what she was saying. She just knew me as Amanda, the bass player's wife. That's it. She didn't know that I had trained myself to fix my hair and makeup without looking in the mirror because I didn't like what I saw.

She told me, "You go home and you look in that mirror like you've never looked in that mirror before and you remember what the Lord did for you. You remember that this isn't you. This is not a part of you. That's dead, and it's like your trying to resuscitate it. You're trying to go back to that way." And I thought, "She doesn't even know me. What?!" Then I thought, "Man, I hope she doesn't tell anybody." I actually hoped no one found out my secret, and I realized that I was beginning to care again. I cared what people saw because I knew I wasn't a cutter anymore. That wasn't me. I wasn't this broken, small person anymore. I knew I was bigger than that.

I couldn't wait for the pastor to finish his sermon and give the altar call. I was like, "I've got to get up there now because God may come and I need to get to that alter to repent for this." But then I thought, "I didn't wait to cut, so I'm not waiting for him to finish!" So, before he even finished preaching, I ran from the front row to the altar. I buried my face and started repenting. My husband came over to me. He knew what was going on so he just started praying over me. The pastor was still preaching, but I heard him say, "This is OK. This is OK. You can do this. I'm not offended." And I was like, "OK, good. I didn't offend the pastor. We're good. We can come back to the church."

At the altar, I started recalling things the Lord had told me, truths that I had to speak out loud to the Lord, like the fact that I was no longer bound to abandonment, suicide, and death because the college ministry leaders had prayed them off of me. I had to literally declare that I was not this small, hopeless person—I was a fighter.

When I got home that day, I put my daughter down for a nap, and my husband took a nap as well because he was working nights. With both of them sleeping, I went into the bathroom to change into comfy sweats and then I remembered the woman's words that pierced so deep inside me. That day I looked in the mirror and told myself that I am *fiercely* and wonderfully made. And at that moment, while looking in the mirror, I saw myself fiercely and wonderfully made! The Lord rose up through me and I grabbed a bright blue dry erase marker and wrote the words that were burning on my lips, "A wise woman builds her house," which is from Proverbs 31. She doesn't tear it down by cutting or dissecting herself from head to toe.

Instead of seeing the reflection of a woman scarred with cuts, the Lord showed me a fighter. He was building a strong-house fighter! As I wrote on every mirror I could find in our house, I felt the pain of abandonment lift more and more with every word. When I got to the last mirror, tears filled my eyes because that burning I had felt before at the campus ministry was there. I felt it all over my body, my mind, and my spirit! The burning just completely saturated all of me, and I realized the burning was the Lord's love. It was literally the heat of Him covering all over me.

I knew in that moment I was completely delivered from cutting. My walls of fear came down, and I was released. I could feel the love of God seeping in and filling every space. To this very day as I write, that verse is still on my mirror as a reminder that the Lord set me ablaze and the enemy wants desperately to put out my flame. I am now totally free from cutting, my birth mother has been miraculously saved and delivered, and we have a great relationship. I have shifted my focus from pain to this great, burning love that the Lord called me into years ago at my bed.

He has made me a lover of life and life abundantly, as I was made for nothing less.

—AMANDA MARR

A promise of deliverance is the first of the seven promises made to the one who loves God, and it is meant to be made personal. I choose to quote Psalm 91:14 like this: "Because I love You, Lord, I thank You for Your promise to deliver me." Amanda's life screamed for deliverance.

What is ironic is that people who cut end up with two types of pain—emotional and physical. It is deceptive for them to think they are trading out emotional pain for physical pain. When I was young, my uncle jokingly used to offer to hit me on the big toe with a hammer when I had smashed my thumb with one (so it would take my attention off my hurting thumb). This seems to be the deceiving logic of cutting—to exchange uncontrollable pain such as abandonment for controllable pain, making the journey from excruciating heart pain to numbness to eventual hardness of heart. Amanda feared that she had become a monster from having been in pain for so long. Our pain is a heavy burden that only Jesus can bear. (See Isaiah 53:4–5.)

Cutting gives a false sense of control. Amanda said, "The emotional pain never actually went away. It kept building." So she really wasn't in control; she was in deception. The lies she believed about the power of cutting were from the enemy. (See John 8:44.)

Another ironic part of this story is that pain was part of the journey *out of* cutting. Amanda experienced a lifestyle of self-induced pain, even to the point of liking when a cut became infected, and then she said listening to worship music to the Lord felt like sandpaper on her heart—a different kind of pain that God used to bring healing.

Even after Amanda was delivered from cutting, when she faced pain she found she had a deep emotional trigger when she herself was about to become a mother. She had to face the abandonment, the mirror, and her scars with the truth of God's Word. Amanda was living a depressed life of gloom and thoughts of suicide, but she decided to take God's Word seriously. When Amanda called on the Lord, His deliverance went to the very core of the problem, and Amanda has a vibrant life now full of the goodness of God.

God is there to deliver us from problems such as cutting and abandonment and the worst possible bondages and addictions. Ever since Amanda could remember, she had struggled with abandonment, but she left church services and Bible studies not surrendered to the Lord, which only led to more problems. We are not helpless against these sorts of things, and no area of our lives is hopeless or beyond deliverance. God wants to rid us of all hurt and abandonment, fear, torment, and bondage.

If any area of your life is plagued by addiction, hurt, or abandonment, it's because Satan knows how powerful you could be in freedom! Remember Amanda's story and refuse to give him the satisfaction of keeping you in bondage.

CHAPTER 17—JOURNAL

This chapter zeroes in on the first of seven promises in Psalm 91:14–16: because we love God, He promises to deliver us. In previous chapters we have discussed several kinds of problems and fears from which we need deliverance. When we feel like life is going to crush us with calamity, we can turn to this important promise to change the outcome. Do you know God as your deliverer?

_____

_____

_____

_____

_____

_____

_____

_____

_____

_____

GOD LIFTS ME UP ON HIGH

Because he has loved Me . . . I will set him securely on high, because he has known My name.

—Psalm 91:14

No Longer Imprisoned by the Past

There's nothing like the feeling you get when somebody frames you at work and your past seems to come back for revenge! A man I'll call Tim was fresh out of the Texas juvenile system where he had spent more than a year after being convicted of criminal activity and stealing. He had given his heart to the Lord during one of the Bible studies held in the prison dorms on Monday nights, and he had made a real change in his life. He served out his time, and when he was released, his record was cleared.

Even with the benefit of a new start, Tim found gaining decent employment to be a challenge. Word got around about his imprisonment, and some prospective employers were turned off by the gang-related tattoos he could not hide. Finally the manager at the Burger King decided to take a chance on him.

Over time, Tim worked his way up to shift manager. One day at work a large amount of money went missing on his shift. The manager asked everyone who stole the money. Even though Tim was walking with the Lord, when each employee was questioned, one by one they pointed at Tim. It seemed the deck was stacked against him.

But the manager did something out of the ordinary. He looked at Tim and said, "I don't believe he did it! Tim, let's pull the security video, and you and I will watch it!" Tim said that when the manager spoke of his confidence in him, it was the first time in his life someone had believed in him.

Together the two men watched the video. It showed the person who had stolen the money as clearly as possible. Tim was totally cleared! But he was grateful to realize that his boss had confidence in him even before anyone had proof that he had made a change in his life. Tim knew in his heart that God had *lifted him up* from where he had been to where he was now.

BECAUSE WE *KNOW* HIS NAME

In Psalm 91:1 God is called "the Most High," revealing that He is the highest being that exists. Consider the significance of being set "securely on high" (v. 14) with the One who is the "Most High." From on high, we have a better vantage point and a better perspective.

God is also called "the Almighty," denoting that He is "all" mighty—the most powerful. In verse 2 He is referred to as "the LORD," revealing His ownership of all things, and also as "my God," revealing His personal nature. Through these four names we see God unveiled in four unique ways to the one who "has known [His] name." The following story is an example of God doing something for you when no one else is able to help you, even when others want to believe in you.

WHEN CIRCUMSTANCES TRY TO
TAKE YOU DOWN, GOD LIFTS YOU UP

A young man I'll call Scott had been hired as the manager of a pizza place by a family friend. He was studying for the ministry and pursuing his bachelor's degree, and working at the pizza place in order to help pay his way through school.

Scott was surprised when a couple of thousand dollars went missing after he carefully had put the money in the safe the night before. Scott suddenly became the chief suspect when the police brought in a lie detector test for the whole shift, and he failed it.

Scott was called in for questioning. He then started fervently praying and said, "God, You are the defense of my life." The Twenty-Third Psalm reso-nated deeply with him during this time. Scott stood on the promise of being led on the path of righteous-ness, and more specifically the phrase "for thou art with me." After he prayed about it all and turned it over to the Lord, he thought it would soon be over, but it seemed to last an eternity.

The next day the accusations escalated when the police captain did the next interrogation. Feeling overwhelmed and stressed by the relentless scrutiny, Scott stopped the interview and appealed for a lawyer.

Even some of the people closest to him started doubting him when he couldn't pass the lie detector test. Scott didn't want to live under suspicion the rest of his life. The owner of the pizza place wanted to believe in Scott and even laughed at how unreliable lie detector tests can be, but things weren't looking good. It seemed the situation was moving from bad to worse. Scott asked for prayer at Bible study, and that night he prayed desperately.

How did it all work out?

When Scott was at his most desperate point, the real thief (another employee) refused to take the lie detector test and fled town. God lifted Scott up above all the pressure of man and circumstantial evidence that had suddenly engulfed him and cleared his name.

—Based on an interview with Scott

In the Bible, Joseph had the same problem as Scott. He was falsely accused, but he had the favor of God on his life, and God kept *lifting* him back up.

Set Securely on High

To be set securely on high is the second promise to those who love the Lord and know Him by name. Often in life we feel a sense of negativity that tries to pull us down. No matter how high we jump, an invisible weight pushes us right back to the ground. Like the undercurrent of the sea, it would like nothing more than to drown us. To combat this constant force seeking to bring us down, we need to understand God's promise to set us on high. He wants to put the power of lift in our lives; He doesn't want us to let our circumstances dictate the way we live our lives.

REJECTION REJECTS LOVE

Did you ever watch the cartoon *Winnie the Pooh* when you were a child? It featured Winnie the Pooh, a bear that loved honey; Tigger, the tiger that bounced on his tail; and Eeyore, the donkey that was always sad. Eeyore was never  happy even though all his friends loved him. I didn't know it at the time, but I was Eeyore. I would walk into a room, and the thoughts were almost instantaneous—"That person doesn't really like you; he's mad at you for what you did last week. Yeah, he says nice things to you, but he doesn't really mean them."

Rejection was so normal to me. I thought everyone lived with these same thoughts and feelings. Rejection started for me as a child. I don't think I remember a time when I didn't feel rejected. My brother and sister always seemed connected to our parents, but I felt like a third party. My parents said I was their favorite, but *I felt* they were closer to my siblings. Thoughts of jealously would run through my mind, *building walls* between me and my brother and sister. This pattern would repeat itself throughout my school years, my time in the army, the start of my marriage, and into college.

Rejection is odd. Looking back now, I realize believing all those lies was foolish, but at the time they felt so real and true. I never loved myself or knew I had any value. I would treat myself badly—and weirdly enough, the people around me would treat me the same way I treated myself. It's odd that a person feeling rejected will do the very things that cause further rejection. This destructive cycle began in my life very early on: I would worry and stress so much about being rejected that I would end up doing things that would cause people to reject me. I put so much pressure on others to accept me that I inadvertently caused the rejection I was trying to avoid.

Having trouble focusing while reading, I began listening to the Bible on audio and things started to change for the better. Mark 12:31 says to *love your neighbor as yourself*. Instead of giving love to people, I was desperate to receive it. Like a starving man, I never could get enough. I started putting emotionally and spiritually healthy people around me. While it was a start, it still wasn't enough. When they complimented and encouraged me, I felt more accepted, but I still left the conversations feeling empty.

I went from listening to the Bible to declaring certain scriptures over my life. "Therefore you are no longer a slave, but a son; and if a son, then an heir through God" (Gal. 4:7). I spoke verses like this when thoughts or feelings of rejection came at me. This journey has been a struggle, even a difficult battle at times, but now I have hope again. Every time I exchange lies for the Word of God, I get stronger; situations that would have taken me weeks to recover from now have little effect.

My last name is King. And as in the verse from Galatians above, I began to realize that God sees me as

a king, a son, an heir. It is mind-blowing to think that
God trusts us enough to call us heirs and kings, but
He does. People used to talk about how much I hung
my head when rejection really gripped me, but now I
can see myself in Christ, *seated on high*. It seems almost
prideful to think this way, but actually it is pride that
keeps us from receiving all God wants to give us.

God truly has become the *lifter* of my head (Psalm
3:3). More and more lies fall off me every day. I don't
identify with them anymore—God's Word is trans-
forming me into a new creation—what God origi-
nally intended. This realization is what allowed me
to start taking the pressure off other people to validate who I was, and I began putting my trust in the
Lord to validate me. How simple this revelation is,
yet how life-changing!

—LESLIE KING

Seeing From God's Perspective

By dwelling and taking refuge in this God named "the
Most High," we place ourselves in a position next to Him.
This position of being *on high with the Most High* is one
of absolute security and safety. Like a father who scoops
up his young child to remove him from danger, the Lord
pulls us up beside Him, so high that harm can't reach us.
Negative circumstances viewed at eye level often give an
overwhelming sense of despair and alarm. Very few see into
the realm above. Only with the Lord can we gain a higher
perspective on our circumstances. We begin both observing
and thinking from a different viewpoint.

For those who don't like heights and shaky situations, Psalm 91:14 is the verse for you. God promises, "I will set him *securely* on high" (emphasis added). That word *securely* literally means you can't be toppled. When you are positioned securely, you have no reason to feel insecure or afraid.

This concept of the Lord lifting us up resounds through the entire psalm as God promises that those who *know His name* (v. 14) are *sheltered with Him* (v. 1) and seated *securely on high* (v. 14), *dwelling* (v. 9) with Him in a place where *no evil* (v. 10) can reach them. And it is emphasized even more when we read in verses 11–12 that even the angels work to lift us!

Paul expands this concept further:

> [God] raised us up with Him [Jesus], and seated us with Him in the heavenly places in Christ Jesus.
> —Ephesians 2:6

What does it mean to be seated with Christ in the heavenly places? When God raised Jesus from the dead, He made Him more important than anything in this world. And He lifts us up to be seated with Him far above the chaos.

How crucial it is to receive this promise from God that He will lift us up on high. The more we know Him personally, the more we will start seeing things as He does, *from on high*.

CHAPTER 18—JOURNAL

This chapter points out that when God wanted to show the people of Israel something important about Himself or His promises, He would reveal another one of His names to illustrate it. And we've learned how *the Most High* seats us with Him *on high.* This secure position changes our perspective so we see things from His point of view. It also places us above the enemy's attack. What does it mean to you to know you are seated with the Most High?

_____

_____

_____

_____

_____

_____

_____

_____

_____

Chapter 19
GOD ANSWERS MY CALL

He will call upon Me, and I will answer him.

—Psalm 91:15

Hanging On

My nine-year-old bull terrier, Abby, has a large spot around her eye, making it look like she came straight from filming a scene from *The Little Rascals*, and she has a personality to match. I brought her with me when I moved to another home, but it was a bit of an adjustment since I had no fence. She had enjoyed a large backyard at the last house, so I kept her moving around the yard on a long runner cable to give her plenty of exercise and stimulation so she wouldn't get bored.

Nothing could have prepared me for what happened one hot summer night. After midnight I felt a strange urge to go check on her, so I went to where I had staked her out for the day. She seemed to be fast asleep underneath the bushes that ward off the Texas summer heat. I thought about moving her to her kennel, but thought she might enjoy a night out. However, something still seemed wrong. When I crawled under the bushes toward her, I found she was hanging on the chain with vines wrapped all around her neck, holding her up on her hind legs. She was heaving, desperately trying to breathe. I was struck with horror at the thought of how many hours she might have been stuck that way. It took all my strength to break her free, vine by vine. Every attempt I made to get my fingers under her collar and give her more air was in vain; it was pulled tight against her throat.

I started calling out to the Lord to help me and give her enough air to hold on. I worked fervently with both hands, but it felt as though it took me far too long to break her free and carry her to the back porch into the light, and even then the crisis was far from over. I had managed to pull her body away from the entanglement, but the vines were tightly wrapped in her collar suffocating her. Dialing with one hand while still pulling at the vines with the other, I called Stephanie, a friend with a calm mind and able fingers. I never quit calling on the Lord.

When my friend arrived in record time, I left her working on the dog while I went to look for wire cutters to get through the cable that had been woven into a noose by Abby's struggling against the vines. It was agonizing to listen to her choking, shallow breaths while our fingers worked to loosen the vines. Stephanie also prayed as she worked, still trying to get her fingers beneath Abby's collar to loosen it even a small amount, all the time cutting away until we pulled off the last vine. Abby was exhausted from her brush with death but finally breathing freely. So many vines had been wrapped around her neck that they looked like a crown with strands three inches thick.

All of this happened just as I was about to leave

on a trip, and it really gave me a jolt. The Lord had been so faithful to me that even after I had locked down the house and prepared for bed, I felt the need to check on my *sleeping* dog. I had never done that before, but the one time it counted, the Holy Spirit nudged me to do it. Not only that, but He helped me break her free from the bushes and loosen the vines, which kept her hanging on while we prayed and worked to save her. She didn't bark for three days.

Today Abby is in the backyard, barking, doing her happy dance, showing me how high she can jump, and prompting me to thank the Lord for hearing my cries.

—Angelia Ruth Schum

God *Always* Answers His Phone

Just think about what Psalm 91:15 is saying to you. Every time you pray, you open up the prayer lines with God. This one promise should keep a believer constantly digging deeper into God's Word. No matter the size of your problem, you can take it to Him, from life-altering events to the smallest moments of your day.

Seek Him with honesty and humility, and He will hear you. God always hears His people when they call out to Him. There is no end to the testimonies of those who received God's help when they called on His name. Keep a record of your prayers and how He answers them; then you can look back and remember His faithfulness.

GOD WANTS TO KNOW YOU *DEEPLY*

Make sure you understand your role in calling on God. He wants you to call on Him in your personal devotional time, which is so important to establish and maintain. Don't leave your house in the morning without spending time with Him. A day without a prayer covering leaves you wide open in the spiritual realm. Even ten minutes of concentrated prayer will make a difference. God cares about you and wants you to call on Him regarding even the littlest details of your day.

Understanding that you can call on God *whenever* breaks the routine of praying rote prayers. It makes your prayer life more fulfilling and meaningful. You will begin to acknowledge the answers He gives you to your prayers. Learn to be open and honest with Him. He already knows your struggles, doubts, and fears, and wants you to speak from the depths of your heart to His heart, as the Word says: "Deep calls to deep" (Ps. 42:7).

CHAPTER 19—JOURNAL

This chapter reminds us that God hears us when we call out to Him. Is there anything you've been unwilling to take to God in prayer? How can you be more open and honest with Him? Do you have a personal prayer time every day?

_____

_____

_____

_____

_____

_____

_____

_____

_____

_____

_____

Chapter 20
GOD RESCUES ME FROM TROUBLE

I will be with him in trouble; I will rescue him.

—PSALM 91:15

LOST AND FOUND

John and I had been dating for five years, and I wondered in the back of my mind when he would ask me the *big question*. I never pressed him, but my anticipation of the day when my title would change from girlfriend to fiancée made me wonder when that special day would arrive.

We went on a tour to Israel, and since John had been to Israel before, he told me he had a very special place to take me: the Mount of Olives. He held my hand and led me to a place where we had a perfect view of the city of Jerusalem, overlooking the walls of the Old City and the ancient Jewish cemetery. As we stood there holding hands, John said he wanted to read me a few scriptures from Zechariah 14: "On that day his feet will stand on the Mount of Olives, east of Jerusalem. And the Mount of Olives will split apart, making a wide valley running from east to west. Half the mountain will move toward the north and half toward the south. You will flee through this valley...Yes, you will flee as you did from the earthquake in the days of King Uzziah of

Judah. Then the LORD my God will come, and all his holy ones with him" (vv. 4–5, NLT).

After reading this, John put his Bible down, took both of my hands in his, looked into my eyes, and said, "Phyllis, we are standing on top of the very mountain where it is prophesied that Jesus will return when He comes back to the earth a second time, and I want to do something at this very place that will seal our relationship for eternity!" Then John got down on his knees and took something out of his backpack. My heart beat rapidly as he held out a beautiful diamond ring and asked, "Phyllis, will you do me the honor of spending the rest of your life with me as my wife?" I was overcome with tears of joy. The man of my dreams had just asked me to marry him. I responded with a loud "Yes!" as he placed the ring on my finger. Then he stood up, dusted off his knee, and held me in his arms as tears rolled down my face. It was the most perfect proposal I ever could have dreamed of!

After that amazing and unforgettable experience on the Mount of Olives, we started to trace the footsteps of Jesus as we walked down the Palm Sunday route and made our way over to the Upper Room, where the Last Supper was held. My life couldn't get any better! Joyfully we continued our tour of Israel. I was snapping pictures left and right with my new iPhone. I had taken well over a thousand pictures, and why not? This was the most wonderful day of my life. We arrived at the second station along the Via Dolorosa, where there were two churches near a Franciscan monastery. I reached into my purse to grab my iPhone. It didn't seem to be where I had just placed it. It must have slipped further into my purse. I quickly pulled everything out of my purse, but it was not there. Fear gripped my heart as I frantically asked John if he had seen my phone. He hadn't seen it, so he began asking me where I last had it. I was in a panic. My phone was gone!

I prayed as John ran back down the path we had been on. After several minutes, he returned, completely out of breath. He had found nothing. My heart sank. I was horrified at the thought of losing the phone with all of the memories from our trip, so I asked him to go look for it again. This time I went with him. We told our tour guide what had happened and asked him what we should do. He told us that iPhones in Israel sold for 3,000 shekels, which was equal to $1,000 in US currency, so the phone was as good as stolen and we should not waste our time. But we both felt strongly that we wanted the phone back, so we asked him where we could meet up with the tour group later so we could go back to look for the phone.

John and I quickly began walking to where I had last seen the phone. My mind started reeling and began to condemn me, and I started feeling hopeless because of all the pictures I feared were now forever lost. My emotions were getting the better of me as I tried to fight off the feelings of worry and guilt over losing the expensive iPhone. I began to remind myself that I had gotten engaged less than an hour ago. Finally we arrived and began searching the churches to see if the phone might have been dropped somewhere. After searching unsuccessfully, we noticed a security guard booth. We spoke with the officer there and told him that my phone was lost or stolen at this location. He asked us for some details about the phone, took down our names, and asked us to leave our hotel information in case it was found. We thanked the security officer and started walking down the Via Dolorosa to reunite with our tour group.

Discouragement started to creep in. Thoughts again tried to enter my mind about how quickly the most beautiful day of our lives had turned into one of the most disappointing. John grabbed my hand and turned me toward him. I was very ashamed and didn't have the courage to look him in the face. He said to me, "Phyllis, this is the happiest day of our lives. We have to get ahold of ourselves and not allow the devil to steal any more moments away from us. We got engaged today! We don't have to allow losing a phone that we can replace to steal any more time from our special day that we will never be able to replace. Let's make the choice not to let this get us down."

As his courageous, faith-filled words charged the atmosphere, I could feel the joy of the Lord return to me. I remembered that John had proposed to me this day! My dream had come true, and it could not have been more perfect. After that, the loss of the phone didn't seem so heavy a weight. I began to say to myself, "Phyllis, you can always replace your phone." John wanted us to pray together before we joined up with the group. He reminded me again, "Phyllis, we're in the very place where Jesus lived and did many miracles. Why don't we pray right now and ask God for a miracle. After all, we're in the land of miracles."

I knew exactly where John was heading, and I set my faith level with his. As he prayed, he said, "Lord, here we are in the land of miracles where Your Son lived and performed many miracles. I thank You, Father, for the blessed opportunity to be able to ask Phyllis to marry me here in Jerusalem, which makes this the happiest day of our lives. But, Lord, the devil has tried to mess with us today, and Phyllis' iPhone has been stolen. We choose not to get angry, discouraged, or disappointed, because we know that You can return the phone. So, Lord, we forgive the person who stole the phone, and we bless him or her right now in the name of Jesus. We ask you to convict that person to return it. We have special pictures on there, Lord, and we serve a God who can do the impossible, so we thank You in advance for bringing the phone back to us. In Jesus' name, amen."

It was a long, trying day, but we were so happy. We returned to the tour bus and went back to the hotel. John's Jewish friend, Avi, whom he had met during his first visit to Israel, was going to meet up with us later that night to take us into the Old City to celebrate our engagement. We took the train into Jerusalem and met Avi at a bagel shop. The next day was Friday, and it seemed as if everyone was in the Old City; it was swimming with people who were having a good time. We walked all around the Old City while listening to Avi talk about her family life: where she grew up in

Eastern Europe before moving to Israel. We walked and talked into the wee hours of the morning.

It was now 2:00 a.m., and transportation to where Avi lived had ceased. We were having so much fun we didn't realize it had gotten so late. Nevertheless, there was nothing to fear. John's hotel room had two beds while mine had a huge king-sized bed. We invited Avi to come back to the hotel and spend the rest of the night with me until transportation had resumed to her side of Jerusalem. She happily obliged, and we took a taxi back to the hotel. The plan was for John to switch rooms with me so that he could sleep in the king-sized bed and Avi and I could share his room with the two beds. We were so tired that we just went into our respective rooms, grabbed our necessities for the night, and switched rooms. We met in passing in the hallway, swapped room keys, and proceeded to each other's rooms for the night.

As I opened the door to John's room, I heard something knock against the inside of the door. Turning, I looked behind the door to see what had caused the noise. To my surprise, my iPhone was sitting on the ground behind the door, as if it were waiting there for me like a surprise gift from God! I was *ecstatic*! The only thing that was missing from the phone was the case. The entire phone was intact with all of my pictures![1]

—Phyllis Charles Douglin

John realized the lost cell phone for what it was. Satan often sends trouble to try to steal the good out of our lives. The timing of this attack against John and Phyllis could have ruined their engagement day. So many aspects of the situation could have spiraled down: They could have fought with each other instead of praying. The sinking realization that all the photo memories of the trip were lost forever could have devastated them emotionally so they had no desire to pray. Instead, John spoke his faith to Phyllis, and she moved from feeling panic and despair to being encouraged in the Lord.

When trouble hits, more often than not we immediately get swept into a whirlwind of defeated thoughts and negative emotions. If we listen to those thoughts and emotions, even our best day can be brought to ruin. The enemy wants to discourage us by telling us the lie that we are powerless to change our circumstances. Instead of feeling helpless, we can call on God, as John and Phyllis did, and He will be faithful to His promise to *rescue us from trouble* (Ps. 91:15).

TAKING OUR TROUBLE TO GOD

God promises to deliver us from trouble when we call out to Him. The number of testimonies about the effect of praying when we get in trouble would be countless. Sometimes people make light of the testimonies of those who cry out in trouble, because they seem to call out to God only when their lives are a mess. But the alternative is worse—failing to call out to Him at all.

Much of human behavior is about escape. Many decisions are just an attempt to escape pain. Too often we try to *escape* the trouble we find ourselves in rather than facing it, yet it actually can be dangerous to use our own escape mechanisms rather than taking our trouble to God.

It's *Not* Luck!

Sometimes a person will attribute a rescue to nothing more than good luck. However, since God sends sun and rain on both the righteous and the unrighteous (Matt. 5:45), there is no such thing as a lucky break. Those improbable getaways are the result of God seeing us in trouble and coming to save us. Imagine a person has an illness that suddenly goes into remission and they call their friend to exclaim, "Boy, I was lucky to get a good report!"

What people attribute to random chance can in reality be the result of someone praying for them—a grandmother, a friend, or even a stranger who saw them passing by in a car and suddenly felt an urge to pray specifically for them. Too often people chalk up a miraculous event to chance or coincidence having them *at just the right place at just the right time*.

The Bible says we all must acknowledge God (Prov. 3:6). We must give Him thanks for His mercy. Acknowledging luck is not acknowledging God. If a close friend did something kind and helpful for us, we would never think of *not* telling him thank you and instead giving the credit to chance. Let's not do that to God. Give God the appreciation He deserves for rescuing you from the trouble you have had in life.

God Is the Greatest Promise

God is there for us when we are in trouble. We can't ask for any greater promise than His availability. The Lord makes us an awesome promise when He tells us that He will be there for us in the hard times of life and even in the messes of our own making. He never tells us, "You are on your own!"

Maybe you've heard this joke: When the pastor was asked if he liked his job, he said, "Yes, I love my job. But I can't stand the people." Where there are people, there is usually trouble. And especially as you are growing up, you will face unique challenges. You may seem to encounter trouble from every direction—grades, relationships, employment, lack of money.

We face multiple troubling situations every day. Jesus almost makes it like a guarantee us to when He said, "Do not worry about tomorrow; for tomorrow will care for itself. Each day has enough trouble of its own" (Matt. 6:34). Trouble in a day and trouble in life—it is such a relief to know that God has promised that when we get ourselves in trouble or the enemy launches an attack against us, He will rescue us.

CHAPTER 20—JOURNAL

This chapter looks at how God delivers people out of trouble when they call out to Him. God promises He will be there for us in the hard times of life and even in the messes of our own making. Reflect on some ways God has rescued you or created a way of escape for you.

_____

_____

_____

_____

_____

_____

_____

_____

_____

_____

_____

GOD HONORS ME

I will rescue him and honor him.

—PSALM 91:15

PROUD FATHER

Before I started following the Lord I felt as if something was missing, even though I had everything a kid could ask for in many ways. My parents were pretty well off—recently they had given me a brand-new Mustang and a Taylor guitar. We lived in a nice suburb, and I had more than I could have ever hoped for. But still something in me wasn't satisfied. My parents had taken me to church as a child, but God wasn't something we talked about much as a family, and I was unsure if my parents knew the Lord. Eventually my hunger for God led me to a Baptist church where I gave my life to Jesus.

After I graduated high school I was accepted into a Christian university a few hours from home. I was ready to start my new life with the Lord.

My first year of college was great! The Lord led me to a group of friends who helped me go to a deeper place with God. I never knew following God could be so fun! I was in the process of getting a DJ job at the local Christian radio station; I was helping lead worship a couple services a week; and I was going out sharing the gospel with my new friends. This was the kind of life I had been searching for.

The school year had come to a close, and instead of going home for the summer, I decided to ask my parents if I could stay and continue working at the radio station and possibly go on a mission trip. My parents were a little nervous about how quickly my life was changing, but they agreed to let me stay for the summer if I found an additional job in a month's time. However, with all the activities I was involved with in college, I let the time dwindle away without doing much of anything to find an additional job. Before I knew it, time was up and I hadn't found a job. I had gotten myself into quite a predicament.

I wanted to stay in my college town and continue serving the Lord, but at the same time I didn't want to disobey my parents and possibly hurt our relationship—because I hoped that they too would come to know Jesus like I had. Time was up.

My parents called to make it clear that I had to come home. I wasn't sure what to do. But at that moment I had to make a decision—either drive home or stay and face the consequences. I had never stood up to my dad before. He was a large, burly man, over six feet tall, and he could easily intimidate most. You know the type—when he shook hands with others, he could easily crack their knuckles if he so pleased. Definitely someone you wouldn't want to say no to. Well, the moment had come.

Now, at this point I could just imagine him

coming down to get me and literally picking me up on his Harley and dragging me back home. The thought was a bit terrifying. Also, I knew my parents had every right to come and get all my belongings and my car. Honestly, my belongings didn't belong to me at all—my parents had given them to me. So my plan was simple: if push came to shove, I planned to drive home, give everything back to my parents, hitch a ride back to my college town, and ride around on my bicycle for the remainder of summer.

I went to some leaders in my life and instead of the two ideas I was debating, they said I should respectfully ask my parents for a week extension to get an extra job. I took a deep breath and made the call. After a very tense conversation, my parents said yes, but the agreement still stood. If I had no job within a week, I was to come home. I agreed.

This time I redoubled my efforts and quickly applied for a job waiting tables to go along with my radio job. Over the next week I ended up landing the job. I let my parents know about it, and they agreed to let me stay over the summer. While this fulfilled our agreement, I felt that I may have really hurt our relationship, and I wasn't quite sure how to fix it.

What God did next really was a gift to me that I will treasure always. Within the month I received a call from my dad. I missed the call, but he had left a voicemail for me. I wasn't quite sure what to think because I hadn't heard from him since I let him know about the job, but I decided to face the conflict and give it a listen. In the voicemail he said he was just checking up on me to see how everything was going and if I was doing good. Then he said to give him a call so we could catch up. I let out a huge sigh of relief that things had not gone the wrong direction.

However, he accidentally forgot to hang up the phone, and I heard him continuing to talk to someone. It sounded like he was in a restaurant. My father said in a light and comical voice that I had stood up to him earlier that summer and told him that I wasn't coming home. After this I heard a pause and then heard him say something that has impacted me deeply. He said he was proud of me because I had stood my ground. Shortly after he said this, the voicemail stopped, and I couldn't help but cry. Hearing him say that meant the world to me, especially after I didn't go home earlier that summer. It not only calmed my fears of hurting my parents, but it also made me realize my father was truly proud of me and I could look at him eye to eye as a man, and he liked it.

Shortly after this my parents and I started rebuilding our relationship and everything was going really well. I finished two more years at the university, and then my dad got sick. The doctors diagnosed him with cancer, and his health started declining. At this time a pastor of mine gave me a word he received after praying. He felt the word needed to be shared with my dad even though it was difficult. So I went to my dad and told him the word. After this I asked my dad a huge question. Up until that moment my dad had never been too interested when I talked to him about accepting Jesus into his heart. But I felt that I should ask him again. This time, though, he said yes! My dad gave his life to Jesus there in that hospital, and it was one of the happiest days of my life. My dad ended up passing away a few weeks later, but I knew he had hope. I could see that he no longer was afraid of death, and that he knew Jesus would be waiting for him now that he was ready.

After my dad passed, the church was filled with his family and friends from work, most of whom didn't know the Lord. The church was brimming full of my dad's friends, and I would be speaking at my father's funeral. I told the story of how my dad gave his life to the Lord and then I asked if anyone would like to do the same. Several people raised their hands, and the whole church repeated the prayer of salvation after me. I am so thankful that my dad accepted Jesus into his heart and God gave me the privilege to share that special moment with him.

Even during one the most difficult times in our family's life, God was there. It would have been easy for my mom to turn away from God when my dad got sick, but she didn't. Instead she accepted the Lord while my dad was in the hospital. My mom had some hard days ahead of her. On one particular day, her birthday, I knew that it would be especially hard for her to come home to an empty house and face the aloneness. So I left college for a day and prepared a dinner for her and gave her flowers and balloons.

Our relationship grows daily; it is such an honor to watch my mother go deeper with the Lord. She is now actively involved in church, constantly telling me everything God is doing in her life. Not all things in life are from God, but He works all things out for good, and that is exactly what God did in my life.

—JONATHON DOBERNECKI

Very few people achieve the kind of honor God promises in Psalm 91:15 to those who love Him. Honor is a very intense subject, and sometimes it calls for a lot of courage. Jonathon honored God in his life by turning to the Lord in high school when his parents couldn't understand his decision to follow the Lord and start attending church. His family watched him closely, and what began as fear and concern over their son's new way of life eventually turned into respect. And after respect, they eventually chose for themselves to honor the Lord with their lives.

Deep within this story is tucked another story of God honoring His son Jonathon by giving him a gift that he will always treasure—a voicemail that allowed him to hear with his own ears his earthly father verbalizing his respect for him during a challenging time within their relationship. This "accident" was a God-incident! God went on to honor Jonathon when He allowed him to be the one to connect his father to the Lord as well as many of his father's friends.

It is easy to make a list of all the types of honor in Jonathon's story:

1. Jonathon honored God by giving his life to Him and choosing to serve Him in any way he could.

2. Jonathon honored God by not wanting to be an irresponsible son.

3. God gave Jonathon a personalized gift of honor when he received his dad's voicemail. Just the right piece of the conversation was recorded on Jonathon's phone. Even though the background noise almost drowned it out, he could hear his father's words. It is miraculous how God arranged such a thing so Jonathon would know in his heart that he earned his dad's respect, even though his dad never came right out and told him.

4. God honored Jonathon when he had the opportunity to lead his dad to the Lord by acting on the word he received.

5. God honored Jonathon in that he was able to lead many of his dad's friends to the Lord at the funeral—men who normally would not listen to the gospel listened to Jonathon.

6. God honored Jonathon when he helped his mom find a walk with the Lord, which helped keep her from falling into a dark place.

In summary, God gave Jonathon gifts of honor that he will carry with him the rest of his life!

As a reader, we can see Jonathon lived his life in a way that pleased the Lord. Jonathon made it a point to undo any *spoiling of himself.* He took on new responsibility.

Instead of demanding more, Jonathon was willing to give his possessions back to his parents. In Jonathon's case, it is understandable that God gave honor in this way, but let's look at a story where God gave honor when the recipient wasn't nearly as gracious or worthy.

The Uniqueness of This Promise

The story of the prodigal son illustrates a demonstration of honor that is mind-boggling. The son was in a far off land; he had wasted his father's money, and he was starving. It doesn't seem like anything more than hunger that first turned the boy's heart toward home. But he comes back home to repent hoping that his father will have enough grace to make him a hired hand. The son didn't even deserve this after his actions—quitting the farm, demanding his inheritance, and then throwing the inheritance away on nothing, making not one meaningful investment, and falling so deep into the mire that he was living his life as a pig would; now he was looking for his father to rescue him from the mess he had made.

After the boy had taken with him *half the value of the farm*, it was amazing that his father had been able to hold the other half of the farm together, not to mention successful enough to still be hiring. However, if this is not stunning enough to take note of it, the truly shocking part is what the father thinks needs to be done:

> But while he was still a long way off, his father saw him and felt compassion for him, and ran and embraced him and kissed him. And the son said to him, "Father,

I have sinned against heaven and in your sight; I am no longer worthy to be called your son." But the father said to his slaves, "Quickly bring out the best robe and put it on him, and put a ring on his hand and sandals on his feet; and bring the fattened calf, kill it, and let us eat and celebrate; for this son of mine was dead and has come to life again; he was lost and has been found." And they began to celebrate.

—LUKE 15:20–24

The prodigal is a biblical example of a son who didn't deserve the honor he received. The boy by all natural justice should have been honored just to have anyone speak to him after what he had done and how far he fell. And deep inside, he knew it.

When the son thought about the option of returning home, he began to practice the words of his apology to his father. He was aware in his heart that his father would have to be really merciful for him even to get the status of a hired hand. When he was feeding pigs, he was a hired man, but when he began to long to eat what the pigs were eating, he knew he had fallen lower than he could ever imagine. Yet upon his return home he was about to get something he really isn't expecting.

When Jesus tells the parable He is describing the type of Father that God is. The story of the prodigal son is full of bestowed honor, but it all starts the moment the boy comes to his senses and starts his journey home to repent. It seems that God celebrates *at any point we make the decision to turn around and follow Him.*

We can see the increased progression of what the father did for his son in this Bible story, and we can see in our own lives that not only does God rescue us but, shockingly, He also honors us.

The *Father runs* to us when we turn around and head home—*while we are still a long way off*—for He has never stopped watching for our return. He *embraces us and kisses us*, as if we were coming home as a war hero or a famous champion. Honestly, there are no words to express what God's honor looks like on us. But there's more. The fact that *He honors us with His best robe, a ring on our finger, and sandals for our feet* lets us understand that every good thing we have in our lives is a gift from the Father. Yet God does not stop there. He *kills the fattened calf* (the one He had been saving or a special occasion) *and has a party with friends* on our behalf.

For God to honor a life is truly stunning!

But again, *the story is not over. When the older son complains, "You have never done this for me," the father doesn't say, "You poor thing! We will have a party for you with your friends the next day after your brother's!"*

The father leaves the younger son's party and checks on his older son's heart. He steps *outside* to entreat the boy to come *inside*. He hears his older son's explosive vent, assures him he knows he has always been by his side, and admonishes him not to focus on self but instead to rejoice over how far his brother has come. And yet the father makes it clear, *"Everything I have belongs to you!"* Amazing words.

The promise of honor is truly a unique offer.

CHAPTER 21—JOURNAL

This chapter discusses the honor God gives to those who love Him. What does it look like when God honors a life?

_____

_____

_____

_____

_____

_____

_____

_____

_____

_____

_____

_____

GOD SATISFIES ME WITH A LONG LIFE

With a long life I will satisfy him.

—PSALM 91:16

SERVING THE LORD is never boring; from my experience it is always an adventure. Since two key ingredients of adventure are danger and excitement, Psalm 91:16 is a very applicable promise for your life. It promises *long life* and *satisfaction*, both of which are essential if you are called to a high-adrenaline, fast-paced life with the Lord.

It makes sense for a psalm about protection to address the subject of a long life, but this verse goes beyond that—God is promising not only a multitude of days, but also a life well lived. Many people have lived long lives, but they weren't necessarily happy. As depressing as it sounds, you have to ask yourself why anyone would want a long life if it is spent in misery and boredom.

Fortunately such a life is not what God wants for His people. He wants us to have adventure, to wake up welcoming each new day instead of thinking we peaked too soon and left our best days behind us. So many people are afraid of boredom, even to the point of doing potentially foolish things to alleviate it. With God, we never need to worry about being bored! True satisfaction comes from the Lord; everything else is temporary.

Don't get tied up in regrets, dwelling on what could have been. It's not too late, and God will not let you languish. He doesn't want your life to be boring any more than you do. Trust in Him and let Him show you how you can be satisfied.

> Bless the LORD…who satisfies your years with good things.
> —PSALM 103:2, 5

In this sixth promise of Psalm 91:14–16, God says He will give the one who loves Him a long, full life. God doesn't simply want us to have a lot of birthdays. He says He will give us many birthdays, and as those birthdays roll around, we will feel satisfied and complete.

Each of us has an empty place inside our heart, and nothing will fill that emptiness except Jesus. Down through the ages people have tried to fill it with different things, but the things of this world cannot bring lasting satisfaction. Only after you decide to follow fully after God and give Him your whole heart will He fill your life to overflowing. Then you will experience a joy you don't even have words to describe.

What a promise—that as you live out a long life, you can be satisfied. What causes satisfaction? Finding and fulfilling God's assignment for your life brings satisfaction, purpose, and loads of adventure.

PEOPLE ARE THE TREASURE

One Thursday night at our college ministry's coffeehouse we were getting ready to do a treasure hunt. A treasure hunt for us is a tool for outreach and witnessing. Our group

would prepare different categories of clues including names, places, locations, physical descriptions of the people, and possible problems the people might have. Then we would pray until we knew to the kind of person we were looking for. We have had amazing conversations with the people we have met on these evenings of finding our treasures!

This night we prayed, and then we began the treasure hunt. I had prayed and written down Home Depot as one of the clues the Holy Spirit had given me, and I also had a clue identifying the appearance and the color of the clothing of the person I would meet. When I arrived at Home Depot, I soon saw a girl in her early twenties working in the paint department who matched the clues I had received. I went over to her, attempted to engage her in conversation, and told her how she matched our treasure hunt clues. Not only did I not get anywhere with her, but she broke out in a profuse sweat. She was so uncomfortable that I walked away and didn't show her the final clue I'd received from our earlier prayer time.

But then I thought, "Why not give it one last shot and ask her about the clue I had in the 'unusual' category?" I went back to her and asked, "Hey, does the word *witchcraft* mean anything to you?" It had been my final clue, and I decided not to keep it from her.

She said, "Yes, I'm a witch, and my grandmother was a witch as well." She immediately shared with me that she was Wiccan. Through this I was able to make a connection with her, and I shared the gospel with her. I remember noting that she was sweating.

> I wasn't sure if she was just warm, or if the gospel I
> was sharing was causing her to sweat as a manifesta-
> tion of her discomfort. She didn't give her heart to
> God that night with me, but I thanked the Lord that
> I had been able to talk to her about the real power
> there is in Christ and for the clues that led me to the
> treasure and the opportunity to plant a seed.
>
> —ADRIAN BILL

Adrian had a very unique experience as he shared the gospel with a person who normally would not open up about what was going on in her life. Much like the story in John 4, where Jesus talked to the woman at the well and told her things about her life, Adrian showed the girl at Home Depot how he had written down specific things about her. When he did, she opened up.

Someone once said, "The best testimony to Jesus Christ is a satisfied customer." I wrote that on a piece of paper and hung it up on my refrigerator for years. It makes a real dif-ference to people when they can see that you are *satisfied with the Lord*.

However, too many people—unfortunately even Christians sometimes—don't have inside themselves a deep satisfaction with the Lord. Since you can't give what you don't have, ask the Lord to do a special work in your heart and bring you to a place of adventure and *deep satisfaction*. Many people live a lot of years on earth, but what counts most is whether they have experienced the soul satisfaction only the Lord can give. Adrian has found that satisfaction in life, and as a result, he is able to share the gospel with unusual people—even witches!

CHAPTER 22—JOURNAL

This chapter considers the satisfaction God brings to our lives. Reflect on what it means to be satisfied with a "life well lived."

_____

_____

_____

_____

_____

_____

_____

_____

_____

_____

_____

_____

I CAN SEE GOD'S SALVATION

I will…show him My salvation.

—PSALM 91:16, MEV

BEHOLDING GOD'S SALVATION

 Mansur and his friend were taking a drive when they came upon a small car carrying a man, woman, and several children; the car was headed straight toward their Jeep. Mansur's friend was at the wheel, and he knew if he stayed on the road, they would crash and more than likely everyone would be killed. Swerving to get out of the car's pathway, the jeep flipped through the air like an acrobat at a circus. Mansur screamed his friend's name just as the jeep rolled grill over taillights. He felt like he was watching a movie in slow motion. With each roll, items were flying out of the jeep. There was no way to come out of this horrible crash. Instantly Mansur's mind began to reel through his past, making him realize the time he'd wasted worrying about trivial things. The girlfriend he thought he loved had broken his heart when she told him she no longer wanted to date him. In a moment's time that relationship seemed to disappear. And now how foolish it seemed that he had worried about how his family would accept his faith. Things that had

seemed so important no longer mattered. With each heartbeat he was sure it was going to be his last.

Suddenly things went into slow motion. The second time the jeep flipped, it hit the ground hard enough to rattle Mansur's bones. Before he could think, the door was torn off as the vehicle flew back into the air. The thought flashed through his mind that this would be the last thing he would experience as a living person. As the jeep made another head-over-end roll, Mansur remembered being a child in his mother's kitchen. He'd been worried about his friend Daniel. "Can Daniel go to heaven?" he asked his mother. Even at this young age, Mansur pondered the deep questions of life.

During the third flip, Mansur almost flew out of the jeep but managed to pull himself back in. He remembered the faces of two friends who had died. He'd been there with both of them and had seen death up close. The fourth time the jeep somersaulted, he wondered why it had taken him so long to tell his friends and family that he'd become a Christian. Love had drawn him to the faith, and he felt the same love wrap itself around him now.

The fifth time the jeep flipped, everything faded away.

Mansur blinked his eyes and noticed something dripping. *Drip. Drip. Drip. Drip.* It took effort to concentrate on the drip. It was oil.

Oil! Car wreck! Fuel! Fire!

Mansur looked around; the driver's seat was empty. Where was his friend? *Get out! Find him.* He fumbled for the seat belt, but it was stuck. Try as he might, he couldn't get it unfastened. That was it—he needed to pray! "Lord, please give me the strength to get this seat belt loose!"

With supernatural strength, Mansur yanked the seat belt out of the frame. As he pulled himself out of the wreckage, he saw that his legs and knees were covered in blood. He had feared that both his legs had been broken when he started to fly out of the jeep. "Lord, please let me stand and get away before this thing explodes in flames!" But as he took his first step, he realized he had no injuries and was fine.

Adrenaline was rushing through his veins.

He was bloody.

He was bruised.

But he was alive.

Mansur's friend lay on the ground a few meters away. "Don't be dead!" he thought. Afraid that he would have to go to his friend's parents and tell them they had lost their son, he prayed under his breath. Mansur stumbled toward his friend until someone steadied him. "It's OK. He's alive. You need to lie down."

Doctors and medics appeared out of nowhere. Moments later, Mansur found himself strapped to a backboard with a neck brace in place. Forced to look up, he realized, "I've only been focusing on my earthly worries, and I've lost all my joy in serving my God." He knew he had been given a second chance.

"You guys are a miracle to be alive," one of the doctors said. "Not only did you all survive, but you wrecked in front of a medical clinic. We watched it happen from the balcony."

As the ambulance screamed out of the darkness,

Mansur prayed. "God, I've changed my mind about how I want to serve You. I want to be in the hardest, darkest places where even the smallest light will make a difference. I realize I've let too many things steal my joy. I haven't lived my faith well, but that is about to change."

—MANSUR ASHKAR

Do our lives need to nearly end before we get serious about our walk with the Lord? In a life-threatening situation, Mansur found the motivation he needed to get right with the Lord. Isn't it strange how pain can make things clearer, but it also can be what drives us away in the first place? When Mansur had his heart broken in a relationship, his priorities had gotten out of line—he had grown numb to the Lord. The wreck was a wake-up call, and Mansur answered it.

A Grand Climax

Psalm 91:16 reveals God's seventh promise in Psalm 91:14–16. His final and most powerful promise is that of salvation. Has there been a moment in your life when you felt you actually beheld the salvation of the Lord?

Each of us has highs and lows. The camp high, the back-to-school low, the mountaintop high, the valley low—what a roller-coaster ride if we always straddle the fence with God! There must be a specific point we come to in life that awakens something within and prompts us to dedicate ourselves to the lordship of Christ.

Seeing the salvation of the Lord involves reaching out

and taking hold of it—making it a part of our lives. Every life includes a moment of epiphany, the greatest moment, the defining moment, that moment that makes us truly alive. I believe that's what this verse is talking about—that moment when everything in us *beholds our salvation*. It begins now but will finish somewhere out in the future.

As a young person, you will be making some of the most important decisions of your life during the next few years. These choices will influence the rest of your life. Choose wisely! Live life like it counts. Live each day in a way that is worthy of the gift God has given you, for He has promised to show you His salvation.

CHAPTER 23—JOURNAL

This chapter describes the seventh and final promise of Psalm 91:14–16: to behold the salvation of the Lord. Has there been a moment in your life when you felt you actually beheld the salvation of the Lord? How can you live life like it counts?

_____

_____

_____

_____

_____

_____

_____

_____

_____

_____

_____

GOD'S COVENANT PROMISE

WE CAN FIND God's promises all through the Bible, but Psalm 91 is the only place where all of His promises of protection are gathered together in one chapter. Psalm 91 is a promise of protection for all of God's people who love Him and trust Him to do what He says. The world gives us 911 as our emergency number to call if we get in trouble, but God has done better than that. He has given us Psalm 91:1:

> He who dwells in the shelter of the Most High will abide in the shadow of the Almighty.

Now that is a true 911 answer!

My prayer is that this book will lead you to study Psalm 91 until *every fear* is driven out of your life. God wants you to know He will be faithful to bring about every one of these promises if you will be faithful to Him. He wants more than anything for you to see and take hold of His salvation.

PERSONAL PSALM 91 COVENANT

COPY AND ENLARGE THIS Psalm 91 covenant prayer to pray over yourself or your loved one—inserting his or her name in the blanks.

_____ dwells in the shelter of the Most High and he/she abides in the shadow of the Almighty.

_____ says to the Lord, "My refuge and my fortress, my God, in whom I trust!" For it is God who delivers _____ from the snare of the trapper and from the deadly pestilence [fatal, infectious disease]. God will cover _____ with His pinions, and under His wings _____ may seek refuge; God's faithfulness is a shield and bulwark.

_____ will not be afraid of the terror by night, or of the arrow that flies by day; of the pestilence that stalks in darkness, or of the destruction that lays waste at noon. A thousand may fall at _____'s side and ten thousand at his/her right hand, but it shall not approach _____.

_____ will only look on with _____'s eyes and see the recompense of the wicked. For _____ has made the Lord his/her refuge, even the Most High, _____'s dwelling place. No evil will befall _____, nor will any plague come near _____'s tent. For He will give His angels charge concerning _____ to guard _____ in all his/her ways. They will bear _____ up in their hands, lest _____ strike his/her foot against a stone. _____ will tread upon the lion and cobra, the young lion and the serpent he/she will trample down.

"Because _____ has loved Me [God said], therefore I will deliver him/her; I will set _____ securely on high, because _____ has known My name. _____ will call on Me, and I will answer _____. I will be with _____ in trouble; I will rescue _____ and honor _____. With a long life I will satisfy _____, and let him/her behold My salvation."

HOW DO I GIVE MY LIFE TO THE LORD?

I F YOU WANT to accept Christ as your Savior, let the following prayer serve as a guide:

> *Lord, I pray that You will come into my heart and forgive me for all my sins. I repent for going my own way in life. I'm making a decision: I want to live for You. I don't want to live a selfish life, and I pray that You will take anything that is not of You out of my life.*
>
> *I believe Your Word and receive the gift You gave of Your Son dying in my place for my sins and ask that He come live forever in my heart. I confess Jesus as my Lord, and I take the challenge to let You do all and anything You want through me. Please give my life purpose and meaning. It is Yours. Thank You for adopting me and letting me call You by the name of Father. I pray that You will give me an exciting life and that You will take all boredom away!*
>
> *Father, in the name of Jesus I pray. Amen.*

NOTES

Introduction: Switch Play

1. Peggy Joyce Ruth, *Psalm 91: Military Edition* (Lake Mary, FL: Charisma House, 2012), ix–x.

Chapter 6: Behind His Shield

1. Ruth, *Psalm 91: Military Edition*, 36–37.

Chapter 12: Unbelieving Believers

1. Bill Johnson, *The Supernatural Power of a Transformed Mind* (Shippensburg, PA: Destiny Image, 2005), 95.

Chapter 15: Authority Over the Enemy

1. Peggy Joyce Ruth and Angelia Ruth Schum, *Psalm 91 for Mothers* (Lake Mary, FL: Charisma House, 2013), 142.

Chapter 20: God Rescues Me From Trouble

1. John and Phyllis Douglin, *Awakened Love* (Brownwood, TX: John and Phyllis Douglin, 2013), 32–50. See also Phyllis and John, "Our Proposal," http://johnphyllis.ourwedding.com /view/6114840742653381/32850860 (accessed March 23, 2015).

ABOUT THE AUTHORS

PROMINENT AUTHOR AND speaker Peggy Joyce Ruth has helped thousands of people to develop a closer love walk with God. Her messages challenge individuals in all walks of life to delve deeper into understanding God's Word. She offers practical principles for applying Scriptures to day-to-day living. After thirty-five years of teaching a weekly adult Bible study and helping her husband pastor in Brownwood, Texas, she now devotes most of her time to speaking engagements, conferences (stateside and overseas), military events, and writing books. You will laugh at the humorous stories as you relate to real-life accounts of God's Word working in people's lives. Her messages are broadcast and streamed on radio and are available on her website www.peggyjoyceruth.org.

Peggy Joyce writes about her daughter Angie: "There is nothing more fun than being in ministry with your children. Many times we share the platform at conferences and retreats. Angie speaks on subjects such as '8 Strategies for Evangelism,' 'Rattle of the Snake (the key to Preventative Prayer),' 'Delivered From the Power of Harm,' 'Adventures and Risks in the Life of a Christian,' 'One Word From

God Can Change Your Life Forever,' and 'God Is the Defense of Your Life.' Both teenagers and adults will enjoy the high adrenaline in her book *God's Smuggler, Jr.*, as she tells about adventures in smuggling Bibles into China."

Angie works in college ministry, overseas mission outreaches, and manages two Christian FM radio stations. She speaks four times a week for a variety of audiences and is an entertaining speaker.

Peggy Joyce Ruth (left) and Angelia Ruth Schum

For speaking engagement information, please call (325) 646-6894. To connect to stream broadcast, go to www .christiannetcast.com/listen/player.asp?station=kpsm-fm or go to our website's homepage at www.peggyjoyceruth.org and push LISTEN NOW.

OTHER BOOKS AVAILABLE

God's Smuggler Jr. by Angelia Ruth Schum

If your life is boring…if you yearn for more—this book is for you! This is the true story of someone who prayed for anything but an average life: "God, never let my life be boring!" You'll be amazed at how God answered that prayer. As the story develops in an exotic place, there is non-stop action with twists and turns as Bibles are smuggled past armed guards into a communist land. This book will challenge you to pray the same prayer without any stipulations.

ADDITIONAL RESOURCES BY PEGGY JOYCE RUTH:

Psalm 91: Real-life Stories (also available in Spanish)
Psalm 91: God's Shield of Protection
Psalm 91: Military Edition Pocketbook
Psalm 91 for Mothers (also available in Spanish)
Psalm 91 for Pre-Teen Youth
My Own Psalm 91 Book for Toddlers
(available in 14 different languages)
Psalm 91 Workbook (For an in-depth study)
Those Who Trust The Lord Shall Not Be Disappointed
Tormented: Eight Years and Back
(the testimony of Peggy Joyce Ruth)

www.peggyjoyceruth.org — (325) 646-6894

EXPERIENCE A PLACE OF
TOTAL PROTECTION
FOR YOUR FAMILY

Enjoy these additional titles in the Psalm 91 series from Peggy Joyce Ruth.
These comforting books are perfect for family, friends, or anyone
who is seeking refuge from life's storms.

**AVAILABLE WHEREVER BOOKS
AND E-BOOKS ARE SOLD**

www.charismahouse.com | www.peggyjoyceruth.org

/charismahouse   www.CharismaDirect.com

SUBSCRIBE TODAY

Exclusive Content

Inspiring Messages

Encouraging Articles

Discovering Freedom

CHARISMA MEDIA

FREE NEWSLETTERS
to experience the power of the *Holy Spirit*

Charisma Magazine Newsletter
Get top-trending articles, Christian teachings, entertainment reviews, videos, and more.

Charisma News Weekly
Get the latest breaking news from an evangelical perspective every Monday.

SpiritLed Woman
Receive amazing stories, testimonies, and articles on marriage, family, prayer, and more.

New Man
Get articles and teaching about the realities of living in the world today as a man of faith.

3-in-1 Daily Devotionals
Find personal strength and encouragement with these devotionals, and begin your day with God's Word.

Sign up for Free at nl.charismamag.com